MW00790440

My First Novel

And What Became of It

The Authors of ChiLibris

My First Novel . . . and What Became of It

The Novelists of ChiLibris

Published by Hunt Haven Press, Clearwater, FL.

ISBN: 978-1961394780

Contents

Introduction

A few months ago, this bit of information came to my email inbox:

> Molecular biologist **Francis Crick**, who famously helped discover the structure of DNA, explains the importance of taking many shots:
>
> "It is amateurs who have one big bright beautiful idea that they can never abandon. Professionals know that they have to produce theory after theory before they are likely to hit the jackpot" (James Clear's newsletter).

After a moment of reflection, I realized the same thing is true in writing. Most of us who've been writing a while have been to writers' conferences where some folks are still working on the same manuscript they've been writing for ten years. They believe it is their magnum opus. And it might be, if they can finish it.

Writers who are serious about being writers, however, know they have to produce book after book after book . . .

I shared that quote with about 300 Christian writer friends and before we knew it, we were sharing stories of how we got started. Of the novels that shall forever remain in a drawer. Of the many mistakes we made before we learned the craft . . . or before we learned to let go so we could move on to something else.

Here are our stories. We offer them to encourage *you* and shine a little light on the writing journey.

Angela Hunt,
For the novelists of ChiLibris

Chapter 1

Hannah Alexander (Mel and Cheryl Hodde)

I (Cheryl) made up stories and poems and songs before I knew how to spell the words I used. Being an only child who lived in the country, I loved that these stories entertained me and kept me company when I was lonely. I never tried to get them published—I mean, I was six, seven, eight—so they were just for fun. In high school, I wrote poetry for the school paper, wrote editorials, and learned to love the movement of words on paper.

Many years later, as an adult, I found myself facing a temptation in my life that I didn't know how to handle. I needed a distraction, so I sat down and started writing my first full-length novel on a legal pad with an ink pen—this was a few years before computers were a thing. The story was a Christian romantic suspense--romance because I always love a happy ending, and what could be happier than a good romance? Suspense because I could never focus enough on straight romance to make a decent story, and I always wanted just a little more excitement. Three months later, much to my surprise, I actually completed the story. I no longer felt the temptation that had first jumpstarted my journey. So in that sense, it worked. Instead of trying to get that manuscript published, I got a new legal pad and began a new novel. I wrote four novel-length manuscripts in that year and continued to write the next year and the next.

It was vital to my growth as a writer to attend as many conferences as possible while I was writing. Friends in the writing world are pure gold. New friends encouraged me to finally try for publication. Some of us started our own local writers group, and we all found support in that.

I sent manuscripts to publishers as I searched for an agent—another piece of advice that I was given. One editor held onto five of my early romantic suspense manuscripts with the intention of publishing one or more of them in their romance line. I was so excited, until one day I received all of them back in the mail with the explanation that the publishing company was closing its doors.

Speakers at conferences taught us that unless you have enough rejection slips to paper a wall, you haven't worked hard enough. I earned that many rejection slips and more, and they kept coming. Oh, I received encouragement along the way, but it did get discouraging to place all my hopes in my work when years went by without a publication.

Fourteen years after beginning my first novel, I had slowed down a bit. I had thirteen novel-length manuscripts waiting for publication. Many speakers at those conferences I attended had stated that once I got the first novel published, the rest of the unpublished work could find a home, as well. So I waited and hoped.

I'd worked part time and full time jobs to support my habit, I'd endured life and death and marriage and divorce. I'd learned that the best way for me to hone my craft was to read a book about novel writing and also to read a well-written novel—not to copy that writer, but to pick up the flow of words in a unique way. I learned to write with a timer, getting as many words down as possible in thirty minutes without stopping to edit. My way to start a new novel was to work on backgrounds of my characters, because whoever they were, the story was theirs, and that's how the book took shape, with character sheets. Other friends found that they worked best by plotting their books before they got to know their characters.

Writing was the one constant in my world while everything changed around me. One Sunday night my pastor came up to me before service and said, "Cheryl, I have a man I want you to meet."

Now, he knew I had no interest in dating again after some of my most recent experiences. "No thanks."

"He's a doctor," Bro Ron said.

"I don't like doctors," I told him.

"He's here tonight," he said. "I'll introduce you after the benediction."

"Don't you dare!"

He laughed. I knew he'd do it. As I made my way to the back of the church to hide, I warned my mother that Bro Ron was trying to set me up with a man. "We have to escape as soon as the final prayer ends," I told her.

We tried. Ron was faster. He grabbed Mel and raced with him to the back of the church before we could step out into the night air.

Despite my reservations, I discovered immediately that this young man was not a smug, self-satisfied person as I had expected. I liked him. But I'd been burned once too often, and didn't want to try again.

It took a few more tries by my pastor and friends in the church staff to get us together, but they were undaunted. One night after church, when a bunch of us met for pizza, the staff surprised me by inviting Mel, and then sitting him beside me. I was gracious. He was adorable.

"You're a doctor," I said, "so could you help me paralyze someone?"

He had these pretty blue eyes that widened at my question.

I realized how that must have sounded. I explained that I was a novelist and was working on a book in which I wanted to paralyze a character. His insight would help me a lot.

He eagerly got with the program and gave me all kinds of good ideas, with varying degrees of damage that could be done. I lost my appetite, but found a good source of information.

We eventually began dating without the pressure of church staff, and a year and a half later we were married. Mel is an ER physician. When he came home after a long day, he would download about different types of cases—never betraying a patient confidence, but giving me case details. I found it fascinating, and because of this information I decided to try writing an ER-type novel with his technical input.

While I wrote the first manuscript in what turned out to be the first medical series, the first stories I had written were accepted and published by Barbour. When it came time to put my name on the covers, I chose to have a pen name that included Mel, since he read everything I'd ever written, encouraged me, and gave me a lot of detail about medical issues in this newest manuscript. Having no children, I identified with Hannah in the Bible. So I chose that name. Mel chose Alexander, since that means servant of mankind. He likes to think that, as a doctor, he does serve mankind. We work as Hannah Alexander.

Soon after the first novel was published, we made

contact with an acquisitions editor at Bethany House, and they purchased a three-book series from us, which became *Sacred Trust, Solemn Oath, and Silent Pledge.* After all those long years of writing, all the other manuscripts I had completed began to sell, and they also began to win awards, which surprised and delighted us.

We now have had thirty-four novels published both traditionally and independently. Mel is now our marketing director. We are Mel and Cheryl Hodde, and our pen name is Hannah Alexander.

Some of the best advice we ever received was to just write. Keep the fingers to the keyboard and write for twenty minutes without stopping to edit. Then rest and do it again. You would be surprised how quickly you can get a thousand words on paper that way.

Because of the changes in the publishing world, we now write, edit, and independently publish our own novels, but I will always be grateful for the struggle to be traditionally published, as that forced me to hone my craft with other writers, to learn from many books on writing, and to take edits to heart when our wonderful editors chose to spend their valuable time and effort on our words.

MEL AND CHERYL HODDE (HANNAH ALEXANDER)
www.hannahalexander.com

Chapter 2

Tamera Alexander

I started writing on a dare.

In 1995, my mother-in-law, Claudette Harris Alexander, shared a book with me, one she thought I would really enjoy. I took one look at the cover and decided it wasn't for me. Plus life was busy with young kids and work. Claudette asked me again—several times—if I'd read it. I responded no, but thanked her *profusely* for the gift (I'm Southern, after all) and assured her I would (eventually). The best laid plans, as they say.

Three months later, Claudette died unexpectedly from a brain aneurysm. She was only fifty-eight. Way too young. Weeks passed, and as I was dusting bookshelves downstairs (we lived in Colorado at the time), I happened across the little novel she'd given me—and immediately sat down and read it.

Claudette was right. I felt an immediate connection with the thread of hope woven through that gentle love story—*Love Comes Softly*, by Janette Oke, originally published by Bethany House Publishers in 1979 (and later adapted for television in the 2003 Hallmark Hall of Fame movie).

Reading *Love Comes Softly* sent me searching for more inspirational fiction, which, back then, pretty much fit on one narrow shelf in a bookstore. Still, I devoured the titles —both contemporary and historical—but gradually found my already strong interest in historical fiction deepening.

Move ahead to 1998, my husband and I are driving back to Colorado from Texas one night when I finished reading a novel and, tossing it in the backseat, I turned to him and said (only joking at the time), "I think I could write one of those." Without blinking, he said, "Well, do it." Competitive at heart, I nodded and said, "Well all right!"

It was a dark and stormy night. A shot rang out!

Picture the iconic image of Snoopy atop his doghouse with his typewriter just tapping away, and that was me. Not surprisingly, I chose the historical genre and went to work.

Over the next two years, I wrote and wrote. And rewrote and rewrote. I was working outside the home at the time, so after putting the kids to bed, I would write from roughly 10 p.m. to 2 a.m. every night, then would get up and start all over again.

I was driven. A woman on a mission.

I also familiarized myself with the publishing market, learning which publisher(s) were accepting historical manuscripts, which might be the best fit for pitching my story. At the time Bethany House Publishers had the proverbial corner of the historical market, so I chose them. Mind you, this was back before a writer required an agent to make a submission to a publisher. Times have certainly changed.

I mailed the printed manuscript—yes, tied with twine like you see in the movies, LOL—and then waited, certain I'd hear something any day. Weeks went by. And weeks quickly turned to months.

I finally received an email from one of the editors who said that while the manuscript held potential, it needed work. She kindly took the time to outline the problems (a sagging middle and an end that frizzled out and stalled, among them), then invited me to resubmit the manuscript once those revisions were made. Still determined, I dove in.

After completing three fairly extensive rounds of suggested revisions (again, no agent, just working with a gracious editor who apparently saw a speck of potential and chose to nurture it), my first novel made it to the final pub board at Bethany House Publishers in 2002—after which I received a *very* kind rejection letter from her. Which I still have.

But kind or not, it was a rejection. And, I won't lie, it stung. Especially after working on the manuscript for almost three years. But I learned something . . .

The sun still rises after a rejection. Life is not over. Not by a long shot. I had learned so much about writing a novel during the rewrites with that editor (*Thank you*, Barb Lilland). So after giving myself time to regroup, I took all of that to heart and determined to set about *seriously* studying the craft of writing. I took local writing classes, joined American Christian Fiction Writers (ACFW.com), found a critique group, etc . . .

Meanwhile, I tucked that first novel away and started on a brand new story (about which I'd dreamed the opening scene—talk about fresh motivation). Once I finished that second novel, I signed with an agent, and we submitted *Rekindled* to Bethany House—who then offered me my first three-book contract for Fountain Creek Chronicles (*Rekindled*, *Revealed*, *Remembered*).

So what happened to that first novel?

Fast forward to 2007, my family and I had recently moved from Colorado to Nashville, my fifth novel is about to release, and my agent calls. "Tammy, Thomas Nelson Publishers wants you to write the first historical for the Women of Faith Fiction line." I explained that with back-to-back books, I had no time. She responded, "This is a huge opportunity, Tammy. Don't you have any ideas? Maybe something you started then stuck in a drawer?"

Yep, that first novel . . .

My agent said the publisher needed the summary ASAP for a meeting the next morning at 10 a.m. So I went searching for the manuscript. I finally found it in the garage. I quickly read through the story—and realized how right that editor had been. Despite my rewrites, that story still had problems. Big ones. So I put the manuscript back in the box and wrote a fresh summary of the story and characters that had lived and breathed inside me for almost seven years. I had a contract the next day and wrote the novel in seven months (my fastest ever).

The Inheritance released in March 2009 and immediately became a CBA and ECPA bestseller. It went on to final for best historical in the 2010 Christy Awards and won the 2010 RITA Award for best historical. Now over 100,000 copies later, it's still one of my bestsellers.

Through all of this, the Lord taught me a lesson I'll never forget . . .

Every "No" along the way is really part of God's final "Yes!" when his perfect timing is reached.

Read that again and take it to heart. It's true in writing. It's true in life. It was true for me and it'll be true for you, too. Give God your dream, and write that novel, first and foremost, for him. For an Audience of One. Then get ready for a journey!

Best writing advice:

Give yourself permission to write badly so you can learn to write well.

Tamera Alexander

www.TameraAlexander.com

Nineteen books and counting!

Chapter 3

Mesu Andrews

I've heard that readers make the best writers—and I wasn't much of a reader—which explains my long-and-winding publishing journey. However, *studying* my Bible is a borderline addiction, which began in the early 1990's with Ann Spangler's, *Women of the Bible,* and Liz Curtis Higgs, *Bad Girls of the Bible.* I loved how they combined Bible study with well-researched short fiction.

Ann Spangler seemed to "crack the code" on Solomon's impossible-to-understand love poem, Song of Songs. How could King Solomon, a guy with six hundred wives and three hundred concubines, know anything about *real* love? Spangler's short story about the "shepherd princess" captured me, and the biblical stanzas began to whisper a never-before-told story.

Every day for a year, I read the Song of Songs' eight chapters, allowing God alone to whisper the meaning of His love story to my heart. A very unique allegory took shape—set in biblical Israel during Solomon's early reign. I wrote it as part study, part fiction and hoped to take the Christian publishing world by storm—like my author-heroes: Ann Spangler and Liz Curtis-Higgs. In the market analysis of my first book proposal, I described the project as a hybrid like: *Hinds Feet on High Places* meets *Bad Girls of the Bible*. But, in truth, no one had ever written anything like it.

Red flag #1.

Off I went to my first writer's conference. My sample chapters had a little Bible study, a little fiction, and a little devotional material. Did it matter that I'd never read a full-length biblical novel? Did it matter that I had no formal literary training or a platform to help a publisher market a book?

Non-fiction newbie red flags #2, #3, #4.

Still, I was certain every publisher at the conference would be eager to contract my innovative approach to Solomon's Song of Songs.

- First critique: Senior Editor, Bethany House Publishers, "You should stick with speaking at women's conferences because you'll never be a writer."
- Second Critique (an agent who was equally brutal).
- Third Critique: Senior Editor, Focus on the Family, "I wouldn't publish a Bible study on Song of Songs by Billy Graham, let alone a pastor's wife with no platform from Indiana."

If there had been a large rock nearby, I would have crawled under it! Instead, I spent the next three days attending only essential workshops and hiding in my room. But Jesus arranged two unscheduled and life-altering appointments.

While walking from a workshop to the elevator (still

trying to be invisible), I recognized a dear friend coming toward me in the hallway. Was I hallucinating? Perhaps the stress had made me as looney as the editors and agent said I was! But no! The friend was John Maust (President of Media Associates International at the time), who had just finished teaching a conference workshop. John's parents served in our church as deacons and was a familiar face in the sea of uncharted waters in which my dreams were drowning. John was my anchor to the "real world" who helped me regain an eternal perspective during the temporal conference.

Fact: *No one ever dies from writer's conference humiliation.*

The second God appointment came with a simple comment from a stranger during the morning devotional time. Wendy Lawton presented a meditation about God's challenge to Joshua: "Be strong and courageous." She urged us to cultivate the same divine strength and courage with our writing. Afterward, I thanked her, and she invited me to attend the Mt. Hermon writer's conference in San Jose, CA. She might as well have invited me to the moon! I had decided to never attend another writer's conference in my life. I was *not* Joshua.

After four years of healing—and shifting my focus to devotional writing—Jesus provided not only the strength and courage but also the finances. I ventured to Mt. Hermon's conference, met DiAnn Mills on the airport shuttle, who immediately helped me find Wendy Lawton. Though I still made newbie mistakes, by God's grace an agent offered representation. She worked for three years to sell my devotional project, but after three years of refusals, we both realized my non-fiction was a dead end.

My critique partner suggested I resurrect the Song of Songs project. "This time you should write it as a novel without the study material."

"Fiction?" I didn't even try to mask my horror. "I'm a serious Bible teacher!"

"Oh, I'm sorry," she said, smirking. "I forgot you were a better teacher than *Jesus*."

I so love her. With her quippy question, she reminded me that Jesus taught with parables. *Story* reaches beyond a cognitive transaction to engage our emotions with memorable concepts. Through my friend's gentle confrontation, she helped me refocus on my purpose and reevaluate the tool to achieve my writing goal. This single conversation was the turning point of my writing career.

I began reading every biblical novel I could find. Unfortunately, the CBA (Christian market) published very few books in this genre during the early 2000's. I read dozens of ABA (general market) stories about the Bible by folks who didn't revere the Truth, so the books tended toward fantasy and/or apostasy. It lit a fire in my belly! Christians needed to write compelling, passionate, and page-turning biblical novels. I needed to write biblical novels!

One problem. My fiction writing stunk.

So, I registered for Mt. Hermon again and, this time, for Gayle Roper's fiction mentoring clinic. On the first day of class, Gayle returned my 10-page submission with red-ink edits that looked like the paper was hemorrhaging! I left class to receive my first critique and started spewing apologies.

"Take a breath." Vicki Crumpton (Revell's senior editor at that time) tried to calm me. "You have some craft issues, but I think you can tell a story."

Craft issues? I didn't even know what POV (point-of-view) meant, but Vicki asked to see the whole Song of Songs manuscript if I promised to work closely with Gayle during our class. Later I discovered that Vicki had come to

Mt. Hermon hoping to expand Revell's biblical fiction presence in the Christian market—feeling the same passion ignited in me years before. A few months later, Revell offered me a contract, and Vicki became my editor. Her PhD in theology helped guide me through some difficult Bible stories, and her gentle spirit provided invaluable training and a priceless friendship.

Because of other books in Revell's publishing pipeline, they wanted to delay publishing the Song of Songs manuscript (released 2012 as *Love's Sacred Song*). So, they offered me a two-book contract and asked that I write *Love Amid the Ashes* (LATA) in the meantime. LATA released in 2011 and by God's guiding hand received the ECPA Debut Novel of the Year!

There have been many hurricanes, squalls, and dry docks during my "publishing voyage." God, in His omnipresence, is always with us yet also waiting over the horizon with a surprise. Publishing is about waiting and adjusting to the out-of-our-control. It's about being teachable. About trusting the Lord, industry professionals, and the passion God places on *our* heart. Most of all, it's about writing for the One who created us—each one uniquely—in His image.

"Whoever gives heed to instruction prospers, and blessed is the one who trusts in the Lord." Proverbs 16:20

Mesu Andrews
www.MesuAndrews.com

Chapter 4

James Scott Bell

I was going to self-publish my first novel, back when self-publishing required skin in the game. You needed plenty of moxie, foolishness, and money. I knew enough not to go with a vanity press, and just enough about the Bill Henderson self-publishing movement to give it a try.

I also knew no publisher was likely to consider a crazy novel that was the confession of a 120-year-old-man who writes about his joining Darwin on his famous voyage, influencing him to come up with the theory of evolution, then going through history like Forrest Gump, spreading it to key people and locations. At that time Christian fiction was pretty much Janette Oke, Frank Peretti, and a few young, perky pre-ChiLibrians.

Through my church I had contact at a publishing house, College Press, that would be present at something called the Christian Booksellers Association Convention, and wangled an invitation to work at their booth. My goal was to talk to Christians in the book publishing game and get some insider tips on how to do it myself.

On the plane to the event, 1994 this was, I started

talking to another passenger on his way there. His name was Roger Elwood, and I knew he had written a Peretti-esque novel called *Angelwalk.* (My wife, Cindy, worked in a Christian bookstore and I always scanned the sparse fiction shelf.) I told him of my plan and he kindly offered to introduce me to some editors on the floor.

One of them was John Van Diest, who'd founded Multnomah, and along with his son had just started Vision House, a new publishing venture. John asked me about the novel I'd written, I told him, and he asked if he might have a look at it. What could I say? I had a copy of it with me and gave it to him.

Two weeks later he called me and said he wanted to publish it.

"Forget it," I said, "I'm publishing it myself."

Um, no. I said something like, "Really? *Really*?"

He offered no advance. But I didn't care. I figured that was a lot better deal than going into debt to pub it myself.

The Darwin Conspiracy came out the next year. I did a signing booth and everything!

The book sold enough copies for me to buy a spa for our back yard. The kids always called it "The spa Dad's book bought."

JAMES SCOTT BELL
www.jamesscottbell.com

Chapter 5

Lori Benton

My first novel, or the first written with the goal of seeing it published, was a fantasy tome based in Iron Age Celtic culture. I wrote it in my early twenties (1990-1994). It's called *The Silver Brooch*. During the mid-1990s, after thumbing through *Literary Marketplace* and other such listings at my local library, I submitted it to several Christian Fiction publishers who accepted that genre (one didn't need an agent then for such submissions).

While I received very encouraging rejection letters, that's all I did receive. While my writing seemed to please there were many structural issues with the book, firstly its length, which was somewhere short of the entire *Lord of the Rings* series but not terribly far off that mark. No surprise there. I'd never read a writing craft book, attended a conference, or even met a published writer before I'd all but finished it.

I've since moved on to other genres (and learned a thing or two about acceptable manuscript lengths though I confess I still struggle and my first drafts are *very* long). Finally, in 2013, I was published as a historical fiction writer with *Burning Sky* (WaterBrook/Multnomah). But in a sneaky way I'm currently reviving that eponymous silver brooch, if not the story itself, and have found a way to slip it into the historical novel-in-progress.

LORI BENTON
https://loribenton.com

Chapter 6

Heidi Chiavaroli

I worked on my first novel for four years. During that time, it underwent many changes—plot changes, POV changes, even a switch of who I had determined were the main characters!

In these four years, I learned a lot by entering contests, joining a critique group, and even submitting and gathering rejections from agents. Eventually, this manuscript even won a contest, but alas, the rejections continued.

I finally asked myself a very difficult question. Was this novel—the novel I poured my heart and blood and tears into—the goal of my writing, or was getting meaningful, hope-filled stories out into the world the goal of my writing?

After much praying and seeking, I found that the latter was my goal. With that clarity before me, I was able to find the courage to move on to a new story.

Over the next decade, there were times I thought I would quit. I assumed I had probably put as many hours into my writing career as a person pursuing their Master's Degree put into their total college education. I refused to see those hours go to waste. Something *must* simply come from them. As a former marathon runner, I hunkered down and kept running the race toward publication.

Although my second novel eventually helped me land an agent, it wouldn't be until Manuscript #6 that I would secure a contract with my dream publishing house. Now, fourteen novels later, I do plan to revisit that first novel and see how I can improve it in order to get it into the hands of my readers!

The best piece of writing advice I ever received was that writing *can* be learned. That was so encouraging to me and kept me focused during this journey.

My dear friends who feel this crazy pull to write . . . if you are discouraged or wonder if this dream will ever happen for you, hold fast. Some make it look easy. But for some of us, God has a different timetable, a different plan. Persevere. Throw yourself into the arms of Jesus. And run that race.

Heidi Chiavaroli
www.heidichiavaroli.com
Fourteen books published to date

Chapter 7

Mindy Starns Clark

Writing is one thing, but writing a novel is something else entirely. At least that's what I was starting to realize as I struggled to make headway in a career that had been floundering since college. I'd always had a knack for telling stories, and I had honed my craft by earning a degree in English with a specialization in creative writing. After graduation, I'd sold some articles and short stories as a freelance author, and I'd found some success as a technical writer, an advertising copywriter, and even a published playwright. But five years after graduating from college, the thing I wanted most was still the one thing that eluded me: to be a novelist. To write novels.

What on earth was the problem? I knew how to write, how to form coherent sentences, even how to create a plot and come up with some interesting characters. I did it all the time in short stories and plays. Shouldn't writing a novel be the same as writing a short story, only longer? The same as writing a play, only in narrative form rather than solely through dialogue?

Apparently not. As it turns out, the novel is a

completely unique art form, a fact that I'd never been taught in any class but eventually heard someone say at a writer's conference. It was at a panel discussion about breaking into the business, and as soon as one of the authors on the panel said it, I sat up and took notice.

"Not only is it a unique art form," another panelist added, "but, unfortunately, about the only way to learn to write a novel is to write a novel." Everyone else on the dais nodded in agreement.

The only way to learn to write a novel is to write a novel? What an odd concept, but one that made sense to me. I certainly hadn't figured it out any other way. Suddenly, I began to feel excited and encouraged—until another of the authors added, "Of course, your first novel won't be any good, because it's mostly one big learning experience. But throw it away and try again, and maybe at that point things will start to fall into place."

Her comment earned gasps from the audience but simply nods and laughs from her fellow panelists.

"I had to throw out my first two novels," said one.

"I've still got my first three in boxes in my garage," said another.

Could it possibly be true? Had these successful authors once upon a time written entire novels and then simply tucked or tossed them away? Worse, could I possibly bear to do the same?

I wasn't sure. But I knew I had to give it a try. Nothing else had worked. It was time to learn how to write a novel by writing a novel. Surely it would come out good enough to be published, no matter what they'd said.

Fortunately, the timing was perfect. I had just wrapped up a job in Louisiana and packed up all of my belongings in preparation to move north to live closer to my then-boyfriend (now-husband) in New Jersey. It struck me that I might never be in a better position to give this novelist thing a shot. What if I postponed my move by a couple of months, I wondered, and focused solely on writing a novel first? My sweet, supportive parents offered to let me stay temporarily, rent free, in a little apartment off the side of their house. My boyfriend, who'd been my biggest fan since college, thought it was a great idea and said he'd be willing to wait if I really wanted to give it a try before moving up.

I did.

What followed were three of the most absorbing, all-consuming, exhilarating months of my entire life. I wrote around the clock, losing myself in the story that I'd been planning and plotting in my mind for years, working and learning and pushing myself to do better, to keep going, to make my dream a reality. At the end of my time, finished novel in hand, I knew two things for certain: 1. That was the most fun I'd ever had in my entire life, and 2. The book was, indeed, pretty bad. It showed sparks of promise here and there—enough to justify a second attempt at some later date—but for the time being, I decided, I would put away that particular dream and focus on the kinds of writing that I was already doing well and getting paid for.

Time passed. One wedding, two kids, and three moves later, I was finally ready to try again. That time around, I didn't have the luxury of a rent-free room and several uninterrupted months to write. Instead, I wrote on the side, in stolen moments of time, often when everyone else in the house was asleep. The process was more prolonged and plodding, but at least it was doable. It was also just as much fun as I remembered.

More time passed, and I kept writing. My first novel had been hammered out on a typewriter, but now I worked at a computer, my beloved Mac 512K, and the manuscript slowly grew. And grew. It featured four different points of view, an international cast of characters, and a mystery set amid the behind-the-scenes excitement and intrigue of the Olympics. I was intent on pumping out a first draft before going back and reading all I had written, but as I neared the climax of the story, I was starting to feel lost in the details. So I decided to print out the entire novel and read it through to that point before continuing onward.

Good thing I did. I can still remember my growing astonishment as page after page slowly emerged amid the clack and whir of the dot-matrix printer—and didn't stop until it reached page 2007. Yes, my second novel was 2,007 pages long, and I hadn't even gotten to the climax yet!

Devastated, I knew what I had to do. With a heavy heart, I backed up the files on floppy discs, boxed them up with the printout and all of my research notes, and put the whole thing on a shelf in the basement. Novel number two was also a wash.

Perhaps a sane person would've given up at that point. But, once again, I knew two things for sure: 1. The second novel, while still not good enough (not to mention *waaaay* too long) was at least much better than the first, and 2. Writing it had once again been a blast. I wasn't about to stop there.

For my third attempt, I took an entirely new approach. Based on all that I'd learned from writing books one and two, I would this time create some sort of structure before diving in head first. I would plan it out more carefully. I would make smarter decisions about what I would and would not include in the story. And I would write not just with my gut but with my head as well. I would do it right this time.

And I did. A good twenty years after graduating from college, I finally typed "THE END" on novel number three, which came in at a much more appropriate length of about 100,000 words. When I was done, I knew two things for sure: 1. This book was good—good enough, at least, to try and get published—and 2. The only thing more fun than writing a novel is writing a novel that will be first in a series of novels.

That's how I pitched it anyway, and that's the deal my agent landed for me: *A Penny for Your Thoughts* was first in a series of five books, titled the Million Dollar Mysteries, which also included *Don't Take Any Wooden Nickels, A Dime a Dozen, A Quarter for a Kiss*, and *The Buck Stops Here*. The series launched my career and nowadays is considered a "cult classic."

Just as I'd been told, I learned to write a novel by writing some novels—and, more importantly, by setting the bad ones aside and starting again until I got it right. Clearly, that was the best piece of writing advice I ever got. It wasn't fast or easy, but in the end it worked for me.

Here's hoping it works for you too!

Mindy Starns Clark

www.MindyStarnsClark.com

More than thirty books, fiction and nonfiction

Chapter 8

Colleen Coble

I can still remember the first story I ever wrote. It was in first grade and was about twin colts. My teacher praised my writing, and the seed was planted. Someday I would have a book in a library! Libraries are hallowed places to me, so that was my goal. That was it—just a single book in a library somewhere. I didn't even care if I donated the book as long as it was on a library shelf.

The seed lay dormant through the early years of marriage and raising a family. We women often put our dreams aside to focus on our families, and that's what I did. "Someday" I was going to write. I devoured books by the armloads from the library, and it bothered me to read the hopelessness in them that assumed there was no God. I wanted to write a story with hope in it—not preachy, but hopeful. But nothing came.

August 28, 1990 changed everything. The phone rang late that night with the news that the oldest of my three younger brothers, Randy, had been killed by lightning in a freak farm accident. As I emerged from the storm of grief, I realized that if I was ever going to follow my dream, I needed to get started. I was approaching my fortieth birthday, and time was marching on.

As part of the grieving process, my husband and I made a trip out to Wyoming to see where Randy had lived with his family for a few years. As I stood on the parade ground at Fort Laramie, the first idea took root and sprouted. The fire of grief and adversity had finally cracked open the seed that had lain dormant in my heart all those years.

I went home and started to write. It took a year to write that first book. I was sure there would be a bidding war! Not so much. It was a lonely journey at that time too. I knew no other writers and talking about wanting to write a novel felt so presumptuous—I was just a farm girl from a small Indiana town. I had no one to advise me, no one to redirect me. When the rejections came, I'd cry a bit then rework the story and send it out again.

It took SIX years of rejections before the call came from Barbour that they were going to publish my first book, *Where Leads the Heart.* I screamed so loudly the cat hid under the bed and wouldn't come out for hours. I called my pastor to tell him the news, but I got his answering machine. I cried and babbled out what was happening. When he listened to the message, he thought someone had died, and he didn't know who to call back! But I discovered when you have a dream, you need to pursue it. You never know what doors God will open for you. When you struggle to do something bigger than you, it strengthens and molds you.

I wrote eighteen novels and novellas for Barbour, but I was a major mystery/suspense reader, and I desperately wanted to try my hand at a romantic suspense. I found a great agent, Karen Solem (she's still my agent twenty-three years later) and she helped me hone that first romantic suspense novel, *Without a Trace*. When it sold to Thomas Nelson, I cried because it was a dream come true. It still amazes me I get to follow the dream God gave me when I was a little girl.

I had no advice when I was writing that first book so let me tell you what I suggest for any aspiring writer: if that first book doesn't sell right away, put it aside. You learn to write by writing. You can circle back to that book later after you learn more. Don't be obsessed with getting that first book published like I was. It will delay your progress.

Colleen Coble
CEO of American Christian Fiction Writers
Colleencoble.com
Seventy-five books

Chapter 9

James R. Coggins

I was not always a novelist. But I was always a writer. Writers write because they can't not write. They are so overflowing with ideas and stories that they just have to write them down and share them. If they don't, they feel they will burst.

I wrote my first novel in high school, but, fortunately for my later reputation as a writer, it was never published. The plot worked, I think, but the characters were shallow and unbelievable. I was too immature to write a good novel. On occasion in later years, I have been tempted to dust off that manuscript and rewrite it. So far, I have been wise enough to resist that temptation.

Over the next quarter-century, I continued to write—poems; short stories; devotional pieces; newspaper articles; editorials, theological reflections, and news stories for the Christian magazine where I was an editor; a doctoral dissertation; scholarly articles; encyclopedia articles; and even some jokes for *Reader's Digest* (which paid far better than any of the other things). But no more novels.

Two things combined to change this. From the time we

got married, my wife Jackie and I would read together at night. (I would read out loud, and she would fall asleep, especially if I was reading some of the things I had written.) Jackie got me interested in reading murder mysteries. We read Agatha Christie, Dorothy Sayers, Ellis Peters, and other great mystery writers, and then we moved on to lesser known writers. What we discovered was that some of them deserved to be lesser known. One night, we were reading a particularly dreadful example. I literally threw the book across the room and exclaimed, "I can write better than this!" My ever helpful wife said, "Why don't you?"

The second impetus came from a different source. I used to take a city bus to work and got to know some of the drivers. It was a small city, and people were friendly. They talked to strangers. One driver, who was evidently not a Christian, found out I was a writer and asked to see something I had written. I realized that almost everything I had written was directed toward Christians, and I had nothing to offer her.

The result was *Who's Grace?* The hero of this murder mystery was John Smyth, a diminutive Christian magazine editor based in Winnipeg, Manitoba—loosely based on my own life as an editor (loosely because I have never solved a murder). It was not an overtly Christian book, but Smyth was a Christian. My hope was that readers would have an experience similar to someone living next door to a Christian and becoming curious about what made him tick.

My first efforts to sell this book over the next couple of years went nowhere. I submitted it to a few publishers. I submitted it to a few literary agents. Nothing. A few half-hearted compliments but no takers.

I was then senior editor of the *Mennonite Brethren Herald*, a denominational magazine. In the course of my work, I had become acquainted with Les Stobbe. He had a Mennonite Brethren background and had been president of Here's Life Publishers, the book publishing arm of Campus Crusade for Christ. The *Mennonite Brethren Herald* had occasionally reviewed some Here's Life books. One day, Les phoned me to ask me for the current address of a Mennonite Brethren leader. We had recently published an article by this man, Les had known him quite well, but he had moved, and Les did not know where he was currently living. I was glad to supply the address. Les and I had also not been in touch for several years. So, while we were talking, I asked Les what he was doing these days. He said he was now a literary agent. I said that was interesting because I had written a novel. He agreed to let me send it to him. I did, he read it, his wife liked it, and he quite quickly agreed to become my agent. Les immediately got to work, and within what was probably only a couple of months, I had a contract with the publisher Les thought least likely to take my book—Moody Press. As that book headed to the press, Moody offered me a contract for two more novels, which became *Desolation Highway* and *Mountaintop Drive.*

Did I become a published novelist because of a chance conversation on the telephone? Was this the culmination of years of hard work honing my writing skills and establishing a public profile? Or was this all due to the guidance and blessing of God? The first two, of course, but most assuredly the third.

Best Advice

There is a story behind this.

Way back when I first finished university, I was unemployed and not sure what direction to go. One morning, I earnestly prayed, "God, what do you want me to do with my life?" It was a rhetorical question. I was not expecting an answer. But immediately, and very clearly and powerfully, the words popped into my head: "Be a writer." I thought, "That can't be it. That's what I want to do."

So, I sat down and typed up an article. Then I phoned the newspaper (the *Hamilton Spectator*) in the city I was then living in. I said, "I've written this article. What do I do with it?" The secretary or editorial assistant I was talking to said, "Bring it down. The op ed editor is looking for an article."

I didn't know what an "op ed editor" was. It's the person responsible for filling the page opposite the editorial page in a newspaper. That page usually has opinion pieces and sometimes letters to the editor.

I took my article down to the newspaper and handed it to the op ed editor. She read it and said, "It's good. We'll publish it tomorrow."

"I thought, "Oh, that's how it's done. You write something and then sell it." Of course, that's not how it is done. The writing life is filled with far more rejections than acceptances, and it was years before I made any real money from writing. But that first sale encouraged me, and, however imperfectly, I have followed that calling ever since.

I sold several other articles to that op ed editor. One day, she gave me the best piece of writing advice I have ever received. The quote was not original with her, and I don't know who said it first. The advice was: "If you want to be a great writer, live deeply."

James R. Coggins

www.coggins.ca

Five novels and one other fiction work

Chapter 10

Susan Page Davis

The first book I ever wrote (and finished) was *The Priority Unit*, in 1999. I had no writers' group, no online support at the time. I sent it off to Christian publishers, having no idea what I was doing. I stacked up quite a few rejections. One editor wrote "While you work has merit, it does not meet . . ." That was enough to keep me writing.

The Priority Unit sat "in the drawer" for ten or fifteen years. I decided to search out publishers that didn't require an agent. My library had a used book sale, and on the table were several dozen small books from Barbour's Heartsong Presents line. I bought a pile of them and took them home. After reading several, I was confident I could write a similar story.

I went to work and soon sent off my first efforts. The required length was 50-55,000 words. Short, but not too short. I was rejected. Dismayed, I tried again. And again.

The acquisitions editor at the time was Jim Peterson. He emailed me and explained that my writing was good, but my heroines were too similar to others they'd published. I needed to get beyond teachers and librarians. Hmm.

Then Jim noted that he bought four books a month for the Heartsong line—two contemporary and two historical. He said he received about 400 proposals per month, and about 300 of those were contemporary. "Write me a historical," Jim advised.

That changed everything. After a great deal of research and other work, I presented him with *Protecting Amy,* set in 1840s Wyoming. This time, I got a phone call.

"Yes, it's really me," Jim said, "and we're buying your book."

I was thrilled. Jim sent me a list of changes I should make, and I set to work again. Silly me, I'd thought that when a publisher accepted your book, they'd publish it just as you'd written it.

Jim passed the revised manuscript on to his wife, Tracie Peterson, who was then the main editor of the Heartsong Presents line. Tracie sent me a six-page list of further changes I had to make. Oh, and she said almost casually, we've lowered the word count to 45-to-50-thousand. You'll have to cut five thousand words from your book."

Aghast, I said slowly, "I'm not sure I can do that."

"Then I'll do it," Tracie said. "I could cut a thousand from the first chapter." (Or words to that effect.)

I almost screamed, "No, let me do it. Please."

Working with the Petersons taught me more than I can ever express about writing and publishing. *Protecting Amy* was published in 2004, and many more followed—more than a hundred novels and novellas since then.

And *The Priority Unit*? After several years, I dusted it off and sent it to the agent I'd acquired. He thought it had promise and sent it out—for more rejections.

Discouraged, I went through it again. I'd learned a lot

about Christian publishing, and I could see a few reasons why it probably had not been accepted. But I had choices now. I could revamp the book to be more mainstream, or I could self-publish. Ten years earlier, self-publishing fiction was frowned upon, but now it was acceptable. I published *The Priority Unit* in 2017, eighteen years after I finished my first novel. It's now Book 1 in a seven-book series.

I've received lots of good writing advice over the years, but aside from Jim's "Write me a historical," I think the best was a simple, "Read, read, read. Write, write, write."

Susan Page Davis
susanpagedavis.com
106 books to date

Chapter 11

Melanie Dobson

My writing journey began in elementary school when our family moved from Chicago to Ohio's Amish Country. We didn't have a bookstore or library nearby, but during the summer months, I'd pedal my Huffy about a mile to the bookmobile and fill my basket with a treasure trove of stories. Then I'd spend the next week adventuring with friends like The Boxcar Children and Bobbsey Twins.

Some weeks I'd finish reading before the bookmobile returned, and as I waited for the librarian to bring more adventures to our country home, I began dreaming up my own stories. Usually a mystery with a girl detective named something wildly creative like Nancy Drew. I never finished writing those stories, but I discovered that I loved creating new worlds with words.

Fast forward about twenty years. God reignited a passion inside me to return to my love of fiction writing and actually finish what I started. That spark began a wonder-filled and terrifying journey as I slowly discovered how to create characters and weave together a plot. As part of my learning process, I highlighted mounds of favorite novels and writing books, attended conferences, and wrote into the evening hours after my day job was complete.

My first manuscript—a historical mystery—took more than a year to complete, but it had a solid beginning, middle, and an end. I was very proud of this story and excited to share it with others. I sent the manuscript out to a number of publishers thinking someone would be equally as excited to publish it, but instead of excitement, I received rejection after rejection. A whole stack of them. No one, I was told, was publishing new historical novelists and my writing needed some serious work. One editor told me that not even a doctor could revive my story.

After those rejections, I wanted to do just about anything except write, but another idea began brewing inside me. And then a third story. For seven years, I continued learning, writing, editing, and submitting my work. Writing became a regular rhythm in my life, and while I was still scared of failure, I realized that I needed to be faithful to what God had called me to do, whether or not I ever published.

In 2003, something marvelous happened in our family. My husband and I submitted the paperwork to adopt a baby, and nine months later, we received a call that a birth mother had selected us. She was due the very next day. God brought Karly rapidly into our lives, and soon after she arrived, I received a call from another young woman who asked if we would be willing to adopt her child as well. In less than a year, God blessed us with two daughters.

During that season, God gave me another story. A contemporary one about adoption. Unlike my other novels, this story seemed to pour straight out of my heart.

After years of writing and rejections and writing again, an editor asked to publish *Together for Good*.

In the midst of revising my debut, I received a contract from a second publisher for another contemporary novel, and soon after that, God gave me the opportunity to fulfill my dream of writing historical fiction with a new publishing house. That editor had a tight deadline, and without all those years of practice, I never would have been able to complete what became my best-selling book.

The best piece of writing advice I ever received was from a well-known novelist who said she was a "horrible writer" but a fabulous re-writer. That gave my inner editor permission to spill out a "horrible" first draft and then edit, tweak, and polish in the rewriting phase to create a publishable story. While the journey to publication felt impossible at times, I'm filled with gratefulness in hindsight for the many lessons that I learned along the way.

Melanie Dobson
melaniedobson.com
Twenty-eight books published

Chapter 12

Robert Elmer

Sometimes you hear people say that beginning writers should "write what you know." And that's pretty good advice, at least to prime the writing pump. Where did you grow up, what are your hobbies, or where is your family from? Let that built-in inspiration drive a story.

In my case, I grew up with stories from my parents and my grandmother, all of whom were born and raised in Denmark.

What was it like to live in a country that was invaded during World War 2, and then suffered under years of difficult occupation? There had to be plenty of stories there. So I used those family stories as a springboard and inspiration for a historical fiction action/adventure book that might appeal to young readers. Of course, if no one else was interested, I figured I could at least read it to my own young children.

That was the start of the "Young Underground" series for middle readers (generally ages eight to twelve). I began with the dramatic true premise of how the Danish people hid and rescued their Jewish population from the Nazis in

1943, adding fictional characters and grounding it in a Christian worldview.

I worked on that story for nearly three years, sometimes in the evening after the kids were asleep, and sometimes on the bus, longhand, on the way to work in the mornings. I knew the basics of writing, since I'd worked as an advertising copywriter and news reporter. But this was different. It took shape gradually.

Once a draft was finished (yes, it was very rough!) I sent sample chapters to all the Christian publishers I could think of. This was in the early 1990s, when many publishers were still open to considering unsolicited manuscripts. What did I have to lose?

But after a while, I started to receive a stream of polite "thanks but no thanks" letters in return. Well, of course. Except one morning, when I received a phone call from an editor at Bethany House Publishers in Minneapolis. When my wife told me who it was, I scrambled out of the shower to take the call.

Could I rewrite the story, they asked, adding a female character? I hadn't thought of that, but of course!

And could I turn it into a series of perhaps four to eight books? Wait. My heart almost stopped. Were they kidding?

After recovering from the shock, I set to work on a substantial rewrite—and eventually on the rest of the series. And after that followed series after series for young readers.

I've loved every minute of the journey, but the Young Underground and its related series (the Promise of Zion) will always have a special place in my heart. Today, young parents and teachers are sharing the stories with yet another generation of young readers.

So one of the best pieces of writing advice I ever

received was “write what you know.” But remember, that’s only a start!

Robert Elmer

robertelmerbooks.com

Around sixty books (I lost track)

Chapter 13

Eva Marie Everson

In early 1997, after a five-year illness that attacked my immune system, I had finally reached the place where I could walk again for exercise. Up until that time, I was pleased if I could make it a quarter mile. Now, I was back up to the four-mile mark I'd been at in 1992.

One afternoon, as I took my walk, the scent of jasmine filled the air, which reminded me of the honeysuckle that grew wild behind my childhood home. *How long has it been,* I wondered, *since I stood in front of a honeysuckle bush, pulled the stem from the little flowerets, and sipped on the nectar?*

I answered my own question: twenty-five years.

What would make a woman leave her Southern home, not to return for twenty-five years?

The question came out of nowhere. Well, not nowhere. My whole life those kinds of questions had given way to stories I created in my own mind and shared with no one. But on this day, by the time I returned home, I had a storyline completely mapped out. I walked into the house, drank some water, then retreated to our home office where

I began to write what would become the second chapter of my first novel.

While penning the first draft, I met a fellow unpublished writer who held such a wealth of information, I asked him, with my husband's okay, if he would read what I wrote and help with some of the details (such as foreign language phrases because he spoke several languages fluently). His editing skills were so impressive, I promised that if I got a publishing contract, I'd make sure his name was on the book's cover.

Then I hit Chapter Nine and found myself completely stuck. Truth was, I had no idea what I was doing. So, I went to the library and checked out several books on writing fiction including *Writing the Blockbuster Novel* by Albert Zuckerman. I nearly devoured that book, taking a notebook full of notes. Armed with real knowledge, I began to write again. I started with a whole new "Chapter One," making my original first chapter "Chapter Two." Because a portion of the story was set in New York City during the 1970s, I interviewed those who lived and worked there during that era. One of my main characters managed a five-star Manhattan hotel, which I knew nothing about, so I interviewed someone who did.

I wrote for a year. In fact, on the evening after I'd typed "The End," I fell into such a deep sleep that when a tornado passed through our area, I slept through it. All along, when asked, "What have you been up to these days?" I'd answer, "I'm writing a novel," to which I'd hear, "Oh, I started a novel years ago . . ." or "Oh, I wrote a novel one time . . ."

And I'd think, "Yeah, well, the difference is . . . Mine will be published."

I don't know *how* I knew. I just knew.

Back in those days, the process was to put the book

proposal (along with a self-addressed stamped manila envelope into another manila envelope), then mail them to a bevy of editors. Having agents hadn't quite become *the thing* in Christian publishing, so we new novelists were on our own. One by one, those manila envelopes came back. Oh, the sadness of seeing your address penned by your own handwriting among the stacks of bills and other correspondence. But I kept myself occupied by writing, writing, writing . . . but this time, nonfiction.

And then . . . one day . . . there it was—a business-sized envelope from a publishing house. Ah, then . . . months of waiting. Finally, as it turned out, the editor who expressed interest left the house, but he took my name with him. He was opening his own agency, he told me, and he really believed in my project. After signing with him, I shared my latest work, which was nonfiction, and told him I was attending the CBA Booksellers' Convention the following month. With his go-ahead, I approached twelve editors. Imagine my surprise when, nine days later, Barbour Publishing offered me my first contract.

Two books later, in 2000, my agent spoke to my editor at Barbour and said, "You know, she's *really* a fiction writer." The editor asked to see the work I'd completed in 1998. He sent the manuscript and, a few weeks later, I was offered my third contract, this one for a fiction title. *Shadow of Dreams* was the first in a successful three-book series written for Barbour.

The best piece of writing advice I ever got wasn't "write what you know" (a phrase I heard *ad nauseam*) but "know what you write." I spent hours upon hours researching what I *didn't* know to make the work authentic. I cannot tell you how many emails and letters I received from people who lived in Hell's Kitchen during the 1970s, each one asking, "Where did you live exactly? I think we might have been neighbors!" Imagine their surprise when they learned that, until 2000, I had never set foot in New York City.

EVA MARIE EVERSON

evamarieeversonauthor.com

Forty-five plus titles to date

Chapter 14

Linda Ford

I did not plan to be a writer. Sure, I loved reading. I read everything from cereal boxes to Zane Grey. I was an adult with a houseful of children when a friend invited me to attend a writer's group with her. Basically, I went to keep her company and to enjoy an outing. At the time I was struggling with half a dozen acting-out teenagers and as I listened to the speaker tell how to organize a writing project, I thought this sounds so . . . so controllable. From that moment, I was hooked, and writing became my go-to place for safety and solitude.

I began by doing interviews and human-interest stories for local papers. Some of these stories were poignant. They fired up my imagination. I could picture a young lady in a sod hut struggling to cope with the unpleasant circumstances. I saw her sitting on a sunny hillside reading her Bible. That's how my first story began. Although I had read voraciously, I knew nothing about structure. And I mean nothing. I don't know where I was during English and Literature classes. Nevertheless, I flew fearlessly into the mist. It didn't take me long to realize I needed to study the craft. I took courses, attended workshops, bought and read numerous craft books, and had my story critiqued over and over. Each time I'd revise it. Again. It should have been enough to discourage me, but I love my characters so I persevered.

I remember sitting in a hotel room with several other authors and reading excerpts and getting feedback. I edited/revised yet again and felt so pleased with one particular sentence that even now, it still sticks in my mind.

I joined Romance Writers of America and attended one of their NYC conferences which was more than overwhelming for a small-town gal. Always hopeful, I presented ideas to editors. I wanted to write romance but more specifically, Christian romance. It was discouraging to learn how small that market was.

Four years after that initial writer's meeting I decided to get serious about learning how to write a novel. There was a 'local' writing group (over three hours away each direction) that was heavy into romance. I needed to learn the craft, so I traveled there monthly. A multi-published author taught a series on crafting a romance. The first thing I needed, according to her, was a very detailed synopsis. Like ninety pages. I tried. Oh, how I tried. It took me a very long time to realize that was HER method which did not make it mine.

Slowly, I learned, and continue to learn. I believe there will always be more for me to know.

I tried submitting my stories a few times, but they weren't ready, and the editors knew it. So, I continued to revise, to learn, to apply. Finally, I sent a story to Barbour Publishing, and it was accepted. That was *The Sun Still Shines*, the first romance novel I had written and finished, and it is my first-ever release. It did indeed have a young woman living in a soddie and later sitting on a hillside to read her Bible. It was released eight years after I started writing.

Twenty-five years later, I re-released it as an Indie author.

At this point in my writing career, I have more than 100 titles published. I have been an Indie author for the past five years. I am grateful I didn't start out Indie because I have learned so very much from the editors especially those working for Harlequin.

I would offer two bits of advice. #1. Take every opportunity to learn. Grow a thick skin and pay attention to advice. #2. Find your own method whether it's developing a detailed outline or jumping off the cliff into the unknown. The only way for you to discover this is to try things. If they don't work, let them go. I am neither plotter, nor pantser. I call myself a planner. I develop my characters and know what their journey is (something like from fear to trust). I do a very short plot, and then discover plot and character as I write. I've tried detailed plotting, but it feels like coloring by number. In other words, it is not the way I work but I had to learn that.

It seems unnecessary to say this but cover your writing and your readers with prayer.

The best piece of writing advice I ever got was something I heard in many workshops and conferences: Never Stop Learning.

Linda Ford
www.lindaford.org
106 published titles

Chapter 15

Cathy Gohlke

When my first novel was finally completed, I hoped to find a secular publisher, intent on getting my YA novel into public schools and libraries. Having no agent at the time, I compiled a list of publishers from *Writer's Market* and submitted queries. Most of those queries surely ended up in slush piles, never seeing the light of day. One reputable publisher, however, liked the story but asked me to rewrite it for a younger readership. I tried—twice—unsuccessfully.

After several months I applied to The Writer's Edge, an online service that, if your work meets their editorial criteria, shares summary proposals and sample chapters of completed manuscripts with the acquisition editors of qualified Christian publishers.

Based on my submission, three Christian publishers contacted me asking to see my full manuscript. Two of those were reputable publishers; one was a vanity publisher.

After reading my manuscript, Andy McGuire, then a fiction acquisition editor for Moody Publishers, offered a contract for my book—a contract I signed on my 50th birthday—proving that we're never too old to step into a dream God places in our heart. That book, *William Henry is a Fine Name*, was published in 2006 and won my first Christy Award the following year. I don't know that *William Henry is a Fine Name* appeared in many public schools, but it did find its way into libraries and the curriculum of some private schools and homeschool programs.

The best writing advice I've ever received came from a newspaper editor. I was writing feature stories for his local paper at the time. He said, "Watch world and national news. Take those stories, those issues, then find and write the local version."

In writing Christian historical fiction, I've paraphrased that: "Watch world and national news and current events. Understand what grieves the heart of God and what makes me pound the table and weep. Search for that story in history—which constantly repeats itself—and write."

Cathy Gohlke

www.cathygohlke.com

Eleven novels published to date

Chapter 16

Louise M. Gouge

In 1984, I was inspired to write my first novel when I observed a man and a boy tossing a football in a field outside my window. With the encouragement of my husband and children, I wrote about a football quarterback who became a Christian and then returned to his ex-wife and son to make up for his failures. Once I finished the book, I decided to take a creative writing class at my local community college to see what I needed to fix in that story. I got caught up in the college bug and went on to earn my creative writing degree at my local university. One of my professors helped me fix many things in my book, the most important being Point of View.

After graduation, I started attending writers' conferences, and wonder of wonders, an editor bought my book! I was so excited and figured I was on my way to fame and fortune. But God had a different plan. That lovely editor's small publishing house went out of business. My dreams crashed. But then, more wonder of wonders, that editor sold my book to Crossway Books, a larger press that published some very famous names. They titled the book *Once There Was a Way Back Home* (1994) and its sequel, *The Homecoming* (1998).

Neither book made a bestseller list, but it was a beginning and it encouraged me to return to college to earn my master's degree so I could expand my worldview and write in more depth. My master's thesis was *Ahab's Bride*, based on *Moby Dick*'s Captain Ahab's "young girl wife." Research showed no one had published a book on this topic, so my story would be unique. Once again, I thought I was on my way to fame and fortune. But God had a different plan. The very autumn after I earned my master's degree, a very large New York publisher published *Ahab's Wife*, a very different telling of the same barely mentioned young girl wife of the aforementioned Captain Ahab. Again, my dreams crashed. Then, again, wonder of wonders, my agent at the time found an editor named Jeff Dunn, who believed in my story. Swimming upstream with some of his colleagues at Cook Communications, he bought and published my three-book series: *Ahab's Bride, Hannah Rose, and Son of Perdition.* Again, my books were not bestsellers, but they won a few awards, and I found my place in the writing world.

I now write for Love Inspired (nineteen books so far), and love every minute of it. But I always go back to God's better plan for me. Because my first two books were written before everybody and his cat had a computer and cell phone, I took them out and brushed them off, added the modern communications stuff, at last combining them into one volume called *Winning Amber*, now self-published with Amazon. I love all of my book "children," but I have to confess my firstborn is my favorite.

Louise M. Gouge
https://louisemgougeauthor.blogspot.com

Chapter 17

Robin Lee Hatcher

I loved books even before I learned to read because I saw my older brother and all the adults in the family reading all the time. So I suppose it was destined I would become a voracious reader. However, I didn't think about writing a book until my late twenties.

An idea was rolling around in my head when several things happened that caused me to decide to put the story down on paper. One of those things was reading a novel and being unhappy with the ending. In March of 1981, I began writing in the evenings on a yellow pad. On coffee breaks and lunch hours, I typed the manuscript on the office typewriter (remember carbon paper and onion skin paper?). By November of 1981, I'd finished writing my first novel.

Using *The Writer's Market*, I mailed my sample chapters and cover letter to 21 publishers (some, I realized later, weren't suitable for the historical saga I'd written). Most of those 21 publisher I never heard from but two asked for the full manuscript. One of those offered a contract. I signed the contract in May of 1982. By that time, I was almost done writing the sequel. The advance for the contracted book never came, and by August, I learned the publisher had gone bankrupt.

I wasn't sure what to do. Was that contract binding if the advance had never been paid? I didn't know, but I got busy writing another book while I tried to figure things out.

In February 1983, I sold both my first novel and its sequel to a small New York romance publisher. I never saw it again until the mass market paperback released in January 1984. There was no revision letter, no request to make changes. There were no line or copy edits. There were no page proofs. When I saw my first novel published, it came with 83 typos that didn't exist in my original manuscript. Otherwise, it came out exactly as I wrote it. Not the best thing that can happen (understatement).

I was green when I made that first sale, and I had no other writers to support my efforts. Writers organizations were few and far between (Romance Writers of America was only two years old when I joined), and the Internet didn't yet exist. Most places of business (including publishing houses) didn't even have computers back then. I didn't attend my first RWA conference until just before my seventh novel released; that was an eye opening experience.

It wasn't until I got an agent and sold to another publisher (after 12 novels with my original publisher) that I received my first revision letter and learned what it meant to be edited. As I tell other writers, all of my mistakes are in print. Don't rush to publish!

My career has now spanned forty years and over ninety published books. I have received many awards, including the Christy, the RITA, the Carol, and the Faith Hope & Love Reader's Choice, as well as Lifetime Achievement Awards from both ACFW and RWA. So despite all my mistakes being in print, I continued to work hard and learn my craft and improve the stories I wrote. And that is true of every successful writer I know, whether their first book was published or they had to wait many attempts beyond that. Press on.

The best piece of writing advice I ever got came many years after I was first published: Write the best book you can and leave the results up to God.

Robin Lee Hatcher
robinleehatcher.com
Ninety books published to date

Chapter 18

Veronica Heley

I well remember the first story I wrote . . .

It was about a boy who saw a man stealing a chunk of wood from a woodpile. When challenged the man threatened the boy, who ran away. The lump of wood was just that; a lump of wood with no distinguishing marks. And the boy was puzzled.

That, of course, was the trouble. I hadn't worked out why the man should steal a lump of wood with no distinguishing marks on it. I think it was something to do with it being hollow . . .? I couldn't work it out at the time.

So I never finished the tale. But it taught me that I need to know Whodunnit before I start on a story.

I was eight years old at the time and didn't write anything else much for years. And when I did, it was my dentist who introduced me to an agent who lectured me up hill and down dale for twenty odd years, until she retired. By that time she'd arranged for the publication of forty-five books, traditionally . . . and I moved on to another agent for another twenty years . . . and now there are eighty-eight books out there and I'm on my third agent, who will no doubt see me out.

I owe a lot to that dentist!

Best bit of advice: "When you stop writing and start editing, you'll be published."

VERONICA HELEY

www.veronicaheley.com

Eighty-eight books published and counting!

Chapter 19

Roxanne Henke

It was 1998 and my youngest child had gone off to college. If I was ever going to have time to write the novel I'd dreamt of writing almost my whole life, it was now.

I sat down and began typing. About ten pages in I looked at what I'd written and thought, "This is boring. And, if *I* think it's boring . . . what will readers think?" I quickly learned that dreaming about writing a novel is a lot easier than writing one.

Rereading those pages I saw I was "telling" the story, not "showing" it. I started over. Once my characters began interacting and talking to each other, the story took off.

"*Took off.*" That makes it sound like writing my first novel was easy . . . no. No, it wasn't. I quickly learned that writing a novel has little to do with inspiration and much more to do with discipline. I set myself a pace of four, double-spaced pages a day, five days a week. The closer I got to the middle of the novel, where all my characters were tangled up in problems, the more I started to doubt my ability to write my way out. And, even more, I started to doubt whether anyone would want to read this "*thing*." What if it was terrible? What if this all was a waste of time? I imagined editors shaking their heads at my words. I imagined readers rolling their eyes. I finally took a recipe card and on it wrote:

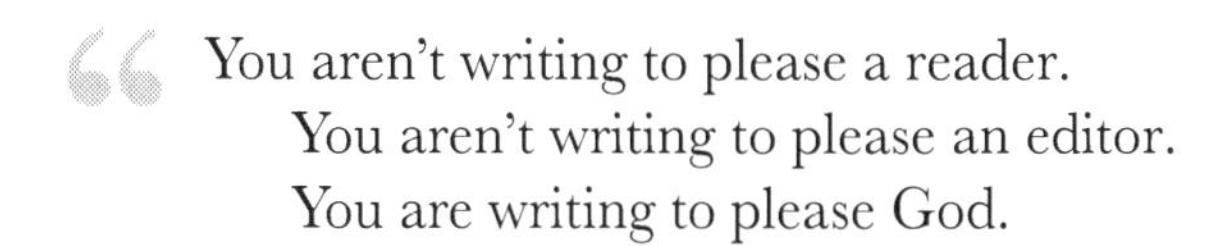

> You aren't writing to please a reader.
> You aren't writing to please an editor.
> You are writing to please God.

I pinned it to my bulletin board in a spot where I read it many times a day. I wrote the middle part in fits-and-starts as my doubts ebbed-and-flowed. Worries crept in. What if I spent all this time writing a novel and then couldn't get it published? What a waste of time. In the end I realized that unless I actually wrote the entire story there would be nothing to *get* published.

I continued typing until one day, about a year later, I typed "The End."

Now what?

This was back-in-the-day when queries were sent through the mail, along with 50 pages, and an envelope with return postage attached.

I made a list of publishers who represented what I'd written and started, one-at-a-time, sending out my packet . . . along with a prayer. With each thick manila envelope that came back was a rejection letter. Some had hand-written notes in the margins. One said, "This is good. I urge you to continue."

Then one day an editor wrote back saying that my manuscript wasn't quite what they were looking for, BUT he knew an editor at another house who he was sure would *love* my story. He told me to send her the entire manuscript (all 350 pages) and he would let her know it was coming with his recommendation.

Elated hardly describes what I felt. I got a manuscript box, wrote a well-crafted query, included return postage (which I was sure I wouldn't need), and sent my "baby" off, along with all my hopes and dreams. And then I waited . . .

One day I got a thin, business-sized letter in the mail from that publishing house. I was positive it was a letter of acceptance. Otherwise, they would have sent my "box" back.

I opened the letter, with a grin on my face, to read these words (along with a few others): *You need to go back and learn the craft of writing.*

What? I read them again. *You need to go back and learn the craft of writing.*

Ouch.

Not only did this editor (apparently) hate my novel, she also kept the manuscript that I had (not cheaply) printed out, and the postage I'd included.

I was so discouraged that I didn't even touch my keyboard for six months. But, God didn't remove my dream or desire. A brochure appeared in my mailbox for a Christian Writers Conference in California. I say "appeared" because, at the time, I didn't even know there was such a thing as a writer's conference. I had no idea how I'd ended up on their mailing list. And, living in rural North Dakota, there was no way I was going to fly to California all by myself to attend a conference with a bunch of strangers. I tossed it in the garbage.

Guess what? A week later a second brochure for the same conference was tucked in with my mail. Without much thought something (or Someone) had me fill out the registration form. At the post office, I dropped it in the mailbox, with a not-small check. If I could have stuck my hand inside the mail slot, I would have grabbed it back out. What had I done? I was petrified.

I'll skip over the part about never flying anywhere where there wasn't someone I knew waiting for me on the other end, and the part about the shuttle bus that was to pick me up not being there . . . and cell phones weren't widespread, not to mention I didn't have one. Eventually, I found the shuttle bus and headed to the conference, telling myself, "They should be nice people, after all, they are Christians." (They were.)

I'd crafted a two-sentence pitch for my novel and that first night, at the opening reception, I spotted the word "Editor" on the name tag of a man standing by the door. I stopped in my tracks and blurted my two sentences. He handed me his card and said, "Send me fifteen pages."

Really? Really! (This man, who would become my editor, later told me that only a handful of the people he tells to send him things, actually do.)

I pitched a couple more editors and was also invited to "send them something."

I sat in on a session taught by the first editor who requested my pages. The three things he said he was looking in a novel were EXACTLY the three main features of my story. After class I went up and told him, "You just described my novel."

He nodded and said, "I already told you to send me a sample."

Okay then.

I attended a "fiction intensive" and the instructor (a best-selling author) described the structure of a good novel and, unbelievably, since I'd never taken a writing class before and had no idea how to plot, the novel I'd written followed that structure exactly.

I made friends at that conference that I still, twenty

years later, stay in touch with. They encouraged me along the way.

Returning from the conference I reviewed my options (hardly believing I had "options") and decided I would send my query to the first editor who'd expressed interest. Off went 15 pages. Within a couple weeks he asked for fifty pages . . . then the whole manuscript. After he read it he told me he was going to give it to another editor whose judgement he valued. He wrote back later saying they both cried (in a good way) over my story. This was the *exact* same story the other editor had so callously rejected.

The next step was to have the marketing department read it. He told me, "Don't get your hopes up, if the marketing department doesn't feel it will sell, we won't publish it."

His advice was too late. My hopes were already soaring.

Within a few days my phone rang. It was "my editor" on the line saying, "We want to publish '*After Anne*.'"

I might have squealed a little . . . or a lot. Maybe I played it cool? I, honestly, don't remember.

He then went on to say, "We'd like to offer you a two book contract. Do you have another novel in the works?"

I didn't. I only had a nugget of an idea but I told him I could send him fifteen pages in a few days . . . and I did.

Within a couple months of that initial conference I was signing a two book contract. I went on to write a total of eight novels for Harvest House. I had the dream of writing one novel God opened the floodgates and had me write eight.

After my eighth book I felt I'd told my stories and told my publisher I was ready to give up my slot to allow another aspiring author a chance to follow their dream.

For the past twelve years I've written a column for the North Dakota Living magazine.

The best writing advice I ever received I discovered on my own: Writing a novel is like a job, sometimes you love going to work, other times not-so-much, but when you've been called to do a work . . . you do it. And, you can't get a novel published that hasn't been written.

Write on.

Roxanne Henke
Roxanne Henke books
Eight novels published
Columnist with *North Dakota Living* magazine

Chapter 20

Pam Hillman

Vroom! **From zero to published in sixty days!**

That got your attention, didn't it? Well, there *is* a bit more to the story . . .

In March of 2011, I had been pursuing publication for almost twenty years, and that's if I don't count the years I had dreamed of writing before I decided to "put up or shut up," as the saying goes. That sounds like a really long time, doesn't it? But when you're working a full-time job and raising a family, then pursuing the writing dream is just part of life. Looking back, the time spent honing my craft, entering contests, submitting proposals and rewrites to agents and editors was time well spent.

So, what changed in 2011?

Digital publishing. But not in the way you'd think. With e-book sales clamoring for its share of sales, publishers, authors, and readers alike were taking a second look at electronic publishing, what we so readily call e-books today. Tyndale House Publishers' answer to that call was their Digital First Initiative.

Tyndale decided to experiment with a new model of

publishing called "Digital First," which is just what it sounds like, a digital-only contract to a handful of yet-unpublished authors. My agent submitted a proposal for *Stealing Jake*, one of my manuscripts that was complete and ready to go. Much to my delight, Tyndale requested the full manuscript a few weeks later. They offered a contract within the month with a release date of July 2011. No, that is not a typo.

Generally, it takes twelve to eighteen months for a print book to hit the shelves, but Tyndale put these e-books on a fast track to publication and had them available in about six weeks, launching the program in July 2011 with four fiction titles and one non-fiction title.

When we submitted the proposal, I didn't know all the details or that the book would be released so soon, but I knew enough to know that what I was experiencing was not the norm, but also exciting, fresh and new, and tied to one of the most established and well-respected Christian publishing houses in the industry.

When I got the call, I'd like to say I screamed and danced around and called all my friends, but I didn't. First of all, I wanted to wait for the contract to be signed. Second, I had a gag order (okay, it wasn't really a gag order, but the term sounds really cool, doesn't it?) on announcing my sale to the world. Tyndale wanted to make a big splash with a press release announcing their Digital First Initiative. Which was a brilliant strategy, if I may say so! Nary a peep from any of the authors or their agents surfaced on the internet until the press release hit the news.

Have you noticed I haven't mentioned revisions yet, and the book was set to release July 1st?

But, alas, no one escapes revisions.

I received my cover in mid-June. What an exciting day! And a few days after that, the revisions came. I had heard horror stories about edits that take weeks, even months, with massive rewrites, so I cleared my calendar in anticipation (dread?) of the edits, but thank goodness they were mostly easy fixes. Tyndale's editors are amazingly talented, and I was spoiled for the rest of my writing life.

While *Stealing Jake* was not my first completed manuscript, it was my first published novel. Tyndale went on to publish *Claiming Mariah*, also as a digital-first e-book. Both books came out in print at later dates. I've had the pleasure of writing more books for Tyndale as well as Barbour Publishing, in addition to independently publishing several novella collections.

On the surface, my first sale seemed fast and furious, doesn't it? But now that you know the rest of the story, you know that I had worked long and hard to reach those sixty days between the contract and publication. My experience is not the norm with traditional publishers since e-books and print books traditionally release at the same time. You might sell your first finished novel, or you might labor in the trenches for years writing many, many stories before seeing your first published work hit the shelves. Just as every story is different, everyone's writing journey is different.

My job—and yours—is to be ready for whatever comes our way.

The best piece of writing advice I ever got was to ***finish the book***. There have been so many gems of good advice I've gotten over the years, but I think that *finishing* is the best advice I can pass on to you, dear reader. Yes, there are some projects that you will set aside because the story just isn't working for one reason or another. But as you grow as a writer, there will come a time when you need to grit your teeth and plow through to the end. Even if it stinks. Then polish it until it doesn't stink. Then do the same thing again, and again, and again.

Pam Hillman

www.pamhillman.com
Sixteen books published

Chapter 21

Angela E. Hunt

I never thought I'd be a writer, but I did take a stab at it in fifth grade. Because I read a lot of Nancy Drew books, my heroine was solving mysteries in her elementary school. Her name was Jade, and she solved the mystery in about ten pages.

I didn't attempt another novel until about 1988. During those in-between years, I started singing, and assume that I'd spend my life in music. Went to college as a music major, went *through* college on a music scholarship, and assumed I'd sing and teach . . . until I was caught in a blizzard. I was singing with a ten-singer group, the Re'Generation, and we were traveling from one gig to another when we got stranded in northeastern Colorado. A wonderful family took us in at two a.m., and we spent the next five days huddling in their home without power, running water, or much food. It was like the TV show *Survivor*, but set in a blizzard.

Anyway, each of us wrote about the adventure in our journals, and when our director caught up to us, he read our accounts. A few weeks later, on an all-night drive, he asked me what I wanted to do when I came off the road. "I guess I'll teach music," I told him.

"You have a way with words," he said. "You should become a writer."

Really? I'd never heard anything like that from my English teachers, but Derric Johnson was not only my director but also my pastor, so I took his advice to heart. Went back to finish my degree, sang throughout my remaining two years, and started studying English. Graduated with an English degree in 1980, and had no idea what I'd do with it.

But the local Christian school had just released a teacher, and they were desperate to find someone to teach 11th and 12th grade English. So off I went, age twenty-two, to teach kids who were seventeen through nineteen. I learned that I *loved* teaching. Wasn't so wild about the disciplining of sassy teenagers, though.

So I went on to work for a church writing curriculum . . . and then became a secretary for a year or two. But the man for whom I worked was a writer, so I typed his manuscripts, watched how he handled interviews, and learned a *lot*. No experience is ever wasted.

My goal was to be a freelance writer so I could work at home when my kids were little. We had decided to adopt, you see, and we worked so hard to get those kids that I didn't want to leave them while I went to work—and I needed to work in order to help put food on the table. My husband, a youth pastor, worked at a job he loved, but I knew he would always have a moderate salary.

So I quit my day job and had business cards printed up. Called some advertising agencies to offer my writing expertise. And was amazed when people actually hired me.

After five *years* of writing magazine articles, catalog copy, and even business letters—earning while I was learning— I saw an ad about a contest for unpublished children's picture book writers. And since I'd never published any kind of book, I went to the library and got a book on how to write a children's picture book. I knew that all writing has a blueprint, and if you want to be published, you *have* to follow the blueprint.

So I sent in the manuscript, waited a couple of months, and finally heard from the editor—out of 500-plus entries, they had narrowed it to twenty-five, then to ten, then to two, and then a nine-year-old boy chose the winner—my book! (God bless that boy!)

So I after writing a few picture books and dozens of magazine articles, I thought I'd try a novel. I had no idea how to start, so I thought I'd write a romance about a woman living in Washington, D.C. I got a book about Washington and a Spiegel catalog. Used a double-page spread of a beautiful bedroom to describe the heroine's room (I'm surprised I didn't include the prices!) Had my heroine meet the hero at several annual D.C. events and quickly realized that my book was missing something—a plot. I put that book in a drawer and didn't pull it out again until the day I tossed it in the trash.

Long story short: I realized there are four stages of learning in any enterprise. First: **unconscious incompetence**. Everybody learns how to write in high school, but professional writing is *not* what you learned there. Adverbs delighted your English teacher, but they will *not* delight your editor. When most people start writing, they have no idea how much they don't know.

Stage two: **conscious incompetence.** I realized pretty quickly that I didn't know much, so I set out to learn it. I studied plots. Characters. Genres. Self-editing. All are crucial to a novel. I read every book I could find on *how to write a novel.*

Stage three: **Conscious competence**. With a few lessons under my belt, I started writing middle grade novels. They had plots. They had characters, including a protagonist and an antagonist. I had learned how to write, but I had to work at it.

Stage four: **Unconscious competence.** I'm not sure anyone ever reaches perfection, but there is a stage when you can write well without overthinking. In any creative field, there's always more to learn. The prose can always be tighter and the characters deeper. The plots can always be improved and the themes better-crafted.

But I love the challenge of working at writing better. Of saying more in fewer words. Of reaching hearts as well as minds.

Pastor Derric taught me something I will never forget. He read the story of King David's sacrifice in 2 Samuel 24, and told us how the landowner offered to donate the sacrificial animals. But David replied, "I will not offer to the Lord that which costs me nothing."

Writing is hard work, even after years of "practice." It will cost you a lot—time, energy, effort, and money. David didn't want to offer the Lord anything less than his best, and neither should we. Our work is our offering to Him.

As we write and rewrite, we conquer the basics and keep moving forward to learn new things. So if you want to be a writer, don't give up. Just get to work.

Angela E. Hunt

www.angelahuntbooks.com

165 books (last time I checked)

Chapter 22

Sunni Jeffers

That first novel. It was 1988, I was forty-two years old, an empty nester, and bored with being a bookkeeper/office manager for our business. I wanted a change but had no idea what I wanted to do. My sister wanted to write a romance novel, so when I saw an ad in the Denver Post for a two-Saturday class on writing a romance, I offered to go with her to the class.

I'd read dozens of romances during the previous two years while recovering from major surgery. I had read one of the presenter's books and loved her sense of humor and delightful style. I had never considered writing. I was surprised to catch the writing bug during those classes. As I listened to her talk about developing characters and settings and plot, a story began unfolding in my imagination. Armed with the notes from her class, I began writing my book on my work computer. It took a year, but I loved the story and the process. The instructor had encouraged us to join Romance Writers of America and enter contests. About the time I completed and revised the book, I saw an ad for a local writer's contest and conference. I printed out all 298 pages and mailed it off to enter the contest. Much to my surprise and delight, I was a finalist. That gained me an appointment with an editor at their conference.

I'm an introvert, but the carrot of the appointment enticed me to attend the conference. There I met kindred spirits who loved reading and dreamed of publishing, and I heard speakers who had achieved the dream. They made it sound possible. Then came my appointment. I clamped down my nervousness and sat across from a woman half my age. She smiled and told me she had read my book and enjoyed it. My hopes rose. Then she said that the story had promise but it was not a romance. It was a coming-of-age story. If I wanted to rewrite it, she would be happy to take another look at it.

I was crushed. I'd gotten it completely wrong, but I loved writing and wanted to be published in romance. I joined RWA and the local chapter and enrolled in creative writing at a Junior College. I tried to rewrite, but the story refused to become a romance. I wrote a different book, and it turned out to be unPC. Who knew a setting of an elk hunting trip in Colorado would be abhorrent to New York publishers? I tried again. Editors loved my story, but I'd mixed too many genres (romance, paranormal, medical thriller, inspirational). I tried again and couldn't get traction. Rejected in front of a group in an appointment at a conference, I walked the halls of the hotel fighting tears and ready to give up. I saw a sign for an Inspirational Romance panel and stepped into the empty back row in a large room. I wanted to disappear, and it seemed like a safe place. At first I just sat, not listening. Then I heard one of the speakers say that our writing could encourage and inspire women in their Christian lives. I was a Christian and my writing already had an element of spirituality.

I went home and revised my current work. I entered

the Inspirational Romance category of Romance Writers of America Golden Heart contest and won. That led to an agent contract, many revisions, and my first contract twelve years after I started.

My first novel? It still resides on my computer untouched for thirty years. Perhaps I should dust it off and revise it – as a coming-of-age novel.

Best advice I ever received was: Write. You cannot revise empty pages. Even one page a day is 365 pages in a year. Anyone can write three chapters. Write chapter four, then five, and keep going. And read. Read fiction and nonfiction and different genres. You never know what will spark inspiration.

I am published under my nickname, Sunni Jeffers, and I'm the author of fifteen traditionally published romance, contemporary Americana, and cozy mysteries and one indie published novel (that romance, paranormal, medical thriller, inspirational).

Sunni Jeffers

https://www.amazon.com/stores/Sunni-Jeffers/author/B001JS69NE

Chapter 23

Jerry B. Jenkins

A hard lesson . . . with my very first novel, *Margo*, back in the 70s:

Like a doofus, I was editing my only copy on a flight to California and left the first half of the manuscript on the plane. It took me two days to track it down with all sorts of desperate phone calls. [Needless to say, I've kept multiple copies of everything since.]

The silver lining, however, was that when I finally reached the woman in the airline's lost and found department, she said, "I'll make you a deal: I'll get you the first half if you'll send me the second."

I could have died and gone to heaven. That remains one of my best "reviews" ever. 😊

Jerry B. Jenkins
jerryjenkins.com

Chapter 24

Jane Kirkpatrick

There were parallels. Though we lived 150 years apart, her name was Jane Sherar and, well, my name is Jane. Her husband was sixteen years older than her and that's the age difference between my husband and me. Both men were builders of barns and houses and roads. Both of us had a dream to build a life on a remote river: the Sherars on the Deschutes River and me and my husband on the John Day River, both in North Central Oregon, both very remote. (Our home was seven miles from the mailbox and eleven miles from a paved road. They lived twenty-five miles from the community of The Dalles.) They were able to accomplish their dreams in the 1860s by living well with their neighbors, the Wasco, Warm Springs and Paiute People. I worked for that tribe. And finally, neither of us had children of our own.

I'd read about Jane Sherar in an historical journal, a piece written by a man then in his 80s but who had won a prize in the third grade for telling the story of his ancestors. I wanted to write a biography of Jane Herbert Sherar but couldn't find much information, her being an ordinary woman and historical women generally being voiceless in newspapers and other historical accounts.

Fiction was an option. A biography tells what someone did and when they did it. Fiction allows exploring why someone did what they did and how they might have felt about it. But someone else needed to write the novel. It couldn't be me because I'd never written fiction. And it couldn't be me because it wasn't my family. And it couldn't be me because I hadn't lived in the region for 100 years. We were new to the area. So the story just swirled around me as I waited for someone to tell this story of a pioneer family and their resilience, their care for each other and the community that supported them.

One day in my musing about how I couldn't tell the story my husband said "If you think it's a great story, you should just write it down. If people don't like your idea, they can write their own version."

Hmmm. But when would I do it? We were "home-steading" our 160 acres, clearing sagebrush, building fences, planting watermelon and grapes. We had to dig a phone line seven miles and did it twice because it didn't work the first time. I was also commuting three days a week driving 2.5 hours on Tuesday morning and staying in a camper a few miles from the reservation then driving home Thursday nights. It came to me perhaps divinely, that all I had been doing between 5:00am and 7:00am was sleeping. I wasn't a morning person, but I thought for the amount of time it might take me to write a book, I could be a morning soul. I planned to set the alarm at 4:00am, be up, showered, dressed, breakfasted and at the computer by 5:00am. I didn't have to write x number of words. I just had to show up.

The next day my husband and I went to an historical society meeting, and I sat next to a man I'd never met. He asked me what I did, and I said, "I'm a writer." It was the first time I said those words without a disclaimer. I'd taken some classes at the local community college, got articles published in a variety of national magazines and newspapers and I'd written a memoir titled *Homestead* and had it published, so I did write. I'd been the administrator of a mental health clinic for seven years and wrote policy letters, too. I could have answered his question claiming to be a mental health professional or a rancher which had engaged me much more. But I said, "I'm a writer" and no lightning came down to strike me for my lie.

"What are you working on?" he said.

"I'm writing the story of Jane and Joseph Sherar and their life with the Wasco, Warm Springs and Paiute People." I had not written a single sentence, but I'd done the hardest work: I'd made the commitment to write that story.

My new friend said, "You should meet my cousin. She owns the property they once homesteaded, and I bet she'd let you walk there."

She did.

Since then, I've written 40 books, most based on the lives of actual historical women and every one of them has had that kind of amazing moment opening doors that I never could have opened. Relatives hearing through the grapevine of my interest and offering to help. Retired loggers wanting to visit libraries to help with research. Someone sitting next to someone else asking if they had information about a certain historical woman discovering a direct descendant who had the family Bible. The incidents stun me constantly.

The lyrical poet Von Goethe in a paraphrase said this about commitment, that what people don't realize is once you make a commitment to something, then Providence moves, and things begin to happen that you otherwise never could have imagined. That word, commitment, comes from the first century banking industry and it means "to make a deposit against which you can later draw." I believe every morning when I showed up by 5:00am to write that novel, I was making a deposit at keeping that commitment.

I wrote a proposal then began showing up by 5:00 am at the computer morning after morning. I worried that getting up so early would make me tired and not able to do the paying work or the hard ranch work. But instead, I was inspired by stepping into another world. I sometimes stretched my time to nearly 8:00am before I had to stop and head for the reservation. The story wouldn't let me go. I was energized for the entire day.

I had an agent, new in the business of agenting (Hartline Literary) and Joyce Hart, who is now retired, sent the proposal to a small publisher in Oregon named Multnomah. (Later Multnomah got bought up by WaterBrook and then Penguin Random House where the book is still in print.) They bought the proposal and contracted with me to write the story. I was 49 years old.

I finished the book titled *A Sweetness to the Soul* about five months later. The publisher liked my title which came from Proverbs 13:19, that reads "Desire realized is sweet to the soul." The book came out in the spring of 1995. Somehow, it got wonderful reviews from *The Oregonian* and other reviewers. That next spring I received notice that the book had won the 1996 Wrangler Award from the Western Heritage and National Cowboy Museum in Oklahoma

City. Previous winners are writers like Barbara Kingslover and Larry McMurtry among others.

Meanwhile, I proposed three books about frontier couples and was signed for the series (I call it a collection) called the Dream Catcher Series. The good news was that I had convinced a publisher I had more great stories to tell, and the bad news was that I didn't know if I could tell them. I had to silence the negative voices saying "Who are you to try to write a story about (put name here); who told you could write? No one will give up cleaning their toilets to read what you just wrote." Each time, each book, requires that commitment.

A funny thing that happened and continues to happen is that almost every morning at 4:00am when the alarm goes off, I have a sore throat. I'm prone to bronchitis and a part of me says I should stay in bed and take care of myself. But I get up to keep that commitment and by the time 5:00 am rolls around, that sore throat is gone. The medical intuit Carolyn Myss says that the throat is the area of commitment. Who knew?

In the year 2000, the Oregon Humanities and Oregon State Library named 100 books about Oregon that were said to be the best stories about the state written in the past 200 years, 1800-2000. *A Sweetness to the Soul* was on that list. It's sold over 50,000 copies but isn't a national bestseller. It has been translated into a dialect of Chinese. Still, I get people who send me a copy of the book and ask me to sign it to newlyweds with the inscription "to be read out loud to each other" or they write other kind things about how the story has touched them from childless to those pursuing a dream. That couple of 150 years ago stepped out of their generation into our own telling us that if we seek a dream with strength, flexibility and faith we can accomplish it and touch the lives of other in the process. It has been the joy of my life to be allowed to tell these stories. It has been a journey sweet to the soul. May you find that joy as well.

Jane Kirkpatrick
www.jkbooks.com
Forty published books

Chapter 25

Harry Kraus

I naturally dropped into writing out of my love for reading fiction. I had an idea for a story and started outlining it on the back of a paper operative note while sitting at the VA hospital in Lexington, Kentucky. It was 1991, and I was a chief resident in general surgery. So yes, it was an insane time to write! I had no time, as I was often in the hospital every other night with clinical duties. I'd never written anything before, not even an article or a short story, but I just had this strong sense that I could write a novel. There are appropriate words to describe me at that time. Insane. Naive. My wife talked some sense into me, while gently encouraging me at the same time. "You have two sons who you never see. What you are writing is as good as what I like to read, but now isn't the time." I looked at my pitiful first computer (a Mac SE30 with a twenty megabyte hard disk and a nine inch black and white display), sighed, and realized she was right. I saved the partial manuscript and returned to it several years later, only after getting out into private practice. With my board examinations behind me, I turned back to my passion and began to write. I finished the manuscript and had only one rejection before being picked up by Crossway Books. The first novel with its humble beginning outside the operating room at the VA hospital, was published as *Stainless Steal Hearts*. I cringe at the title now, but hey, at the time, I thought it was catchy.

Over the years, I've worn two hats, one, a surgical scrub hat, and two, well, I actually don't wear a hat when I write! Since then,I've had fifteen traditionally published novels, and two that I've put out on Kindle as self-published projects. I have three published works of non-fiction, and multiple projects in the pipeline as my agent shops for a new home for my fiction. I'm busy writing a medical mystery series with titles based on the Greek alphabet, beginning with *The Alpha Deception*, *The Beta Score*, and *The Gamma Dilemma*. There are twenty-four letters in the Greek alphabet, so I'll be at this for a while. I'm currently writing the ninth book in the series, *Not One Iota*. It's wacky, comical, and contains the signature medical realism that all Kraus novels contain.

The best writing advice I ever got came from Frank Peretti. My maturity as a writer was actually hampered by my easy path into publication. Because I had a willing publisher, I never read what the fiction teachers were saying. I just wrote by instinct. Fortunately, most of my instincts were solid, but I certainly had room for improvement. Frank Peretti sat with me at a writer's conference, and said, "you're breaking the rules here, Harry."

I looked at him, dumbfounded and naive. "What rules?"

He avoided the eye-roll he should have given me, but I heard a little exasperation tickling at the edge of his voice. "Don't be afraid to read what the fiction teachers have written."

I took his advice. I starting devouring fiction craft books, and became intimidated and afraid that I couldn't write according to the rules. At that point in time, I had four published novels under my belt and a contract in hand for another. But the advice paid off, and the first novel I wrote following the rules, *The Chairman,* was nominated for a *Christy Award.*

I write under my own name, although my agent is shopping the current series under a different pen name. Writing fiction isn't for the faint of heart, but the road is worth following if you have the fire. My website, named Cutting Edge Fiction, is www.harrykraus.com.

HARRY KRAUS
www.harrykraus.com

Chapter 26

D'Ann Mateer

I always knew I wanted to write novels, but through high school and college, even finishing a short story felt hard. Why? Because it never felt good enough. I'd usually abandon it long before "the end."

In January of 2000, my grandmother passed away—my storyteller grandmother. So many of her stories of our family filled my head and begged for release. But instead of simply trying to write a novel, this time I decided to learn a bit more first. I enrolled in a couple of online fiction writing classes through UCLA—yep, all the way back in 2000! I learned a lot about what it means to craft a novel. So much so that I realized how much I didn't know yet, and I abandoned the story based on my grandmother's stories, realizing I didn't yet have the skill to tell it as well as I wanted to.

In the fall of 2001, a friend I'd met in those online classes told me about Nanowrimo. National Novel Writers Month (Nanowrimo) wasn't anything super formal at the time, just the challenge to write 50,000 words in November. I figured I'd give it a try, even though

November held Thanksgiving and my commitment to chaperone 5th graders to an outdoor camp for three days.

Instead of trying again with my grandmother's story, I decided to use the advice my history professor had given me when I told him my ultimate goal was to write historical fiction. "Steep yourself in a time period," he said, "then write from what you know about the people who lived then."

What period of history did I know that well? The American Revolution. I'd always been drawn to that era and my senior honors thesis in college was on Abigail Adams. And so I began, holding only the germ of a story idea, one that combined the history I knew with some of my own struggles over the previous few years. Then I pounded away on the keyboard of my large desktop computer every moment I could.

I made the 50,000 words.

I wrote "the end."

An entire novel. My very first one.

But what to do next?

In a nutshell, my husband saw an announcement about a local Christian writers group in the area and encouraged me to go. There I met my now 20+ year critique partners.

In 2004 I attended Mount Hermon Christian Writers Conference with them. I took my Nanowrimo manuscript, which they had critiqued and I had revised. I met with agents and editors.

An agent asked for my full manuscript. I mailed (yes, *mailed*) her the entire book. Which she rejected.

As she should have. I know now how much of a mess it was. But she'd apparently seen *something* in my work that caused her to ask for it.

That was enough to encourage me to keep going. So I

wrote another novel. And another. And another. And another.

Ten years after finishing my first novel, my dream publisher released my first published book. And guess what the story was? An iteration of that first novel I tried to write, the one based on my grandmother's stories!

What happened to that original novel? It's still in my computer. I still love the basic story. But the work of completely re-writing it (it needs much more than just a revision!) has kept it untouched. So far.

What was the best writing advice I received in that process? Keep writing.

I wouldn't be published today if I hadn't put it into practice.

D'Ann Mateer (originally published as Anne Mateer)
www.dmateer.com
Nine books published

Chapter 27

DiAnn Mills

In 1996, my husband said to me, "Stop telling me someday you're going to write a book. Do it now. Quit your job. I give you one year to get anything published." My youngest son was a senior in high school. I'd been a closet writer all my life, but I was afraid to get started. Afraid of failure. Afraid of not having the right skills. Afraid I was too old to begin a new career.

I wanted to write. Could taste the words. "I believe in you," he said.

I accepted the challenge and devised a plan to work smart and effectively. I looked at my writing goals like a full-time job. If I were to reach the ultimate of publication, I'd have to soar to the top of slush pile. My day was organized into writing, studying how-to books, reading in my genre, and exploring what conferences would teach me the most and provide exposure to agents, editors, and other writers. I started a writer's critique group that met for over ten years.

During the first year, I wrote devotions, articles, a short story, and a historical novel. I experienced rejections along with publications, but I never went back to my old job. In 1998, Barbour Publishing released my first novel. Oh, the excitement of tearing into the box of author copies. The cover . . . the book's name . . . my name. A dream come true, and I never returned to my old job.

That was a lot of books ago, and the process hasn't gotten easier. Social media rose into the publishing world. Every novel is a little tougher to write. The characterization must be deeper. The plot twists and turns to unexpected and unpredictable trails. The setting more intense and antagonistic. The dialogue and emotions swing like a deadly sword fight.

Techniques and tools of the craft weren't immediately drop-shipped into my brain. I experienced lots of deletes and rewrites. Still do! Writing is about hard work and sacrifices.

A commitment to writing means getting started now. The older we get, the more wisdom is packed into our heads. We may need to organize our time and develop a writing space while learning how to professionalize our work. Let others know you're entering a new career, a special interest that's not just a hobby. Join a writer's group and put your work out there to be critiqued.

Coretta Scott King said, "I learned that when you are willing to make sacrifices for a great cause, you will never be alone."

DiAnn Mills
diannmills.com

Chapter 28

Tom Morrisey

My first novel was Stephen-King-esque. Translation: I shamelessly stole every device I could find in King's books, including the one about having no idea how it would end.

I no longer do that — neither filching Mr. King's devices nor writing a book with no end in sight (I actually still believe Stephen King is under-appreciated for the quality of his prose, but think it utter madness to begin a book without knowing how it will end).

My novel was about a bunch of graduate archaeology students on a dig on an Indian mound in Ohio. An American fort had been built atop the mound during the War of 1812. The fort, the students know, was abandoned during the war — its garrison fleeing in fear — although the fortification was never under attack by the British.

In the process of the dig, the students discover a burial site containing the remains of a woman, a skeleton in which every major bone was broken postmortem, and which is covered by numerous decomposed bags of healing herbs, and a broken birdstone (an atlatl counterweight usually found only in the graves of individuals who were held in great esteem).

It turns out they have uncovered the grave of a woman who was possessed by a demon — a succubus who visits in dreams in an attempt to seduce the protagonist, a grad student who functions as the program's photographer and scientific illustrator.

Nope; I wasn't saved yet.

While my graduate degrees are an MA in English with a concentration in early 20th century fiction, and an MFA in creative writing with a concentration in fiction, both earned on teaching fellowships, I supplemented my stipend during my MA studies by working as a scientific illustrator and photographer for my university's anthropology program. The work was interesting enough that I audited some graduate-level classes in archaeology and anthropology.

So, I was able to lace tons of realism into the early chapters of this novel, including one based-on-fact incident in which, as leader-on-duty at a dig one day, I reported the discovery of interred remains (state law required us to do so) and deeply disappointed the loaded-for-bear young homicide detective who responded to the call, when I told him that, as we had radio-carbon dated an artifact in the strata above the grave, we could say with absolute certainty that the death had occurred at least 700 years earlier.

Then, I disrupted this detailed and realistic world by introducing spirits, specters, and sex-crazed phantoms.

My agent at the time was an older gentleman who represented and managed a number of Detroit-area sports celebrities. In the process, he had brokered a number of book deals, and one of the editors he had gotten to know was Michael Korda, the legendary editor at Simon & Schuster. Michael liked my book (it was a partial) and while he admitted it would be an uphill battle, said he wanted to present it to his pub board. He thought he would be able to get us a modest (for Simon & Schuster) deal. This was, as I recall, late summer, 1994.

Hallelujah. Strike up the band. I started to spend money I had not yet earned.

Then, about ten days before the pub board met, Michael got the results of a biopsy back, learned he had advanced prostate cancer, and departed on extended medical leave. I imagine that, in the rush to re-distribute his work, manuscripts already purchased and in process got top priority, while partial manuscripts from unknown, would-be novelists got whatever the opposite is of priority.

Pub board passed on my book.

After this emotional roller-coaster, I decided that, as I was making a modest living with magazine features writing and book-length nonfiction, I would just stick with that.

Then, two years later, I accepted Christ as my savior. Shortly after that, editor extraordinaire Dave Lambert decided he would pass on a book of essays I'd submitted to him, but earnestly asked me to come up with and propose an idea for a novel.

On a visit to HarperCollins Zondervan, I pitched an idea to him literally while we were standing in the airlock between Zondervan's lobby and the parking lot. While we stood there chattering (it was really cold outside and close to freezing in the airlock) he said he'd buy it. That book was *Yucatan Deep* (published by Zondervan on September 1, 2002) and, while it had a smattering of archaeology in it, it was 100% succubus-free.

By the way, the best piece of writing advice I ever received came from the popular crime writer, Elmore Leonard. We both taught one year at the Jackson Writers Conference, and exchanged our latest at a book signing.

The next morning, he said that he had read my entire novel the evening before, and he was effusive with his praise.

I told him, "But, Elmore, I'm pretty sure that novel violates every single one of your 'Ten Rules for Good Writing.'"

He laughed and said, "Probably! But, you knew what you were doing. If you know what you're doing, you can violate every writing rule that there is, and it will still be good."

Tom Morrisey
www.storytellingkeys.com
Nine traditionally published novels to date

Chapter 29

Nancy Moser

The process of getting my first book published is directly intertwined with my testimony of finding God—again.

I grew up going to church but had a very one-sided relationship with the Almighty: He gave and I took. I would check in with Him periodically, always keeping my foot in the door just in case I needed Him. My husband and I were C&E Christians—Christmas and Easter, and often not Christmas as we were really busy with three kids.

Back in the early nineties, after getting a degree in architecture and working as a bookkeeper, I decided I wanted to write novels and be rich and famous (hey, why not?) So I dove in with no training whatsoever and wrote four secular novels. I tried to get them published by sending letters and chapters out to agents. I wrote about murder, adultery, and greed because that's what I thought readers wanted. Dozens of rejections followed. I always gave myself ten minutes to cry and pout but then I'd send my proposal out again. I was nothing if not persistent. I never once considered that it might be *God* telling me **No**.

During these years I subsidized my novel aspirations by writing inspirational humor essays; kind of like Erma Bombeck with a spiritual point. Many of these were published in religious magazines for $10-20 a pop—*if* I got paid. My family went in the hole every time we went out for a celebratory dinner.

Everything changed on March 14, 1995 when I got a non-form letter rejection from a New York agent. It said, "Though other people may find your heroine humorous and charming I find her tedious and boring." It was a knife to my heart. He didn't like my writing style, which was a lot harder to fix than if he hadn't liked other details of my proposal. It hit me hard yet I was determined to make him like my writing. I took the chapters he'd read and began to edit, determined to completely rewrite them.

An hour in I discovered something surprising: the chapters weren't perfect but they were good. They were *me.*

Totally confused, I went on errands. I happened upon a Christian bookstore and went inside. I'd never been in such a store before. A woman, Shirley Bowden, asked if she could help me. I asked if there was such a thing as Christian fiction. She showed me hundreds of books in all types of genres. My heart started beating wildly. Writing *Christian* fiction would mesh with the inspirational humor I *was* getting published way better than my murder, adultery, and greed novels that were going nowhere.

After buying a few books, I drove home. On the way I had a dramatic He-and-Me talk with God. I ended up dedicating all my writing to Him—even though I didn't know Him very well.

The next Sunday I wanted to go to church, but my family balked—after all, it wasn't Easter or Christmas. I couldn't argue with them, but did take our ten-year-old daughter with me. The sermon was about the prodigal son. It was meant for me. I'd come home.

So began my immersion into all things Jesus. I read the Bible through in many versions, listened to Christian radio, read Christian books about knowing God, and read Christian fiction. I also set aside my four novels and deemed them practice. I needed to start fresh.

Soon I got the idea for a new story about four people who receive an anonymous invitation to go to a specific town on a specific day. Their lives would be changed. On the invitation was the mustard seed verse, Matthew 17: 20: "If you have faith as small as a mustard seed and say to this mountain 'move from here to there' it *will* move. Nothing will be impossible to you." That's all I had as I began to write. I handed the invitation to four characters and let the story unfold.

I wrote *The Invitation* in four months. It didn't just unfold, it *flowed.* Once it was done I sent query letters and chapters to Christian book publishers. I got some rejections —which was especially disappointing because I'd naively thought since I was writing what God wanted me to write, the first publisher would take it. *Ha* on me. But eventually I got a letter that asked to see the entire manuscript. I was so excited! I printed it off, packed it up, and sent it on its way.

So began the waiting. It was extra hard because I couldn't send the manuscript anywhere else until this company said yay or nay to it. Usually they responded in two or three months. Usually. Not in my case.

When I was four months in I was getting antsy as patience was not, and is not my virtue. One day as I stretched out for a nap I prayed, "Lord, when will I get a yes on *The Invitation?*" I went to sleep and had a vision: I was looking down on the couch where I was resting, but I wasn't there. Then a light shone down on one of the toss pillows and the number "15" appeared. I woke up. I remembered my pre-nap question. When would I hear? On the 15th!

On the 15th I made sure I was near a phone all day, ready for the call. It didn't come. I was devastated. But then—optimist that I am—I realized God didn't say *which* 15th. *It's next month on the 15th*. But on that 15th there still wasn't a call. So much for visions.

During my waiting time I did two things: I started a sequel to the first book called, *The Quest.* And I learned how to pray. I prayed standing up, sitting down, yelling, whispering, demanding, begging, submitting . . . every which way. As the months stretched into a year I had lots of practice.

In July I finally said, "Lord, *The Invitation* is Yours. Do whatever You want with it." Three days after I surrendered the book I got the phone call I'd been waiting for. Multnomah wanted to publish it! As I was talking to the editor I mentioned that I'd written a sequel. They were tentatively interested.

A few days after the call I realized it had been exactly 15 *months* between when I'd sent the book away to the phone call! Yet I was very glad God hadn't lit up that pillow with "15 months" when I was only four months in. I would have given up. Which shows that we need to trust Him. God knows how much information we can handle, and His timing is always perfect.

The Invitation was the first book in a three-book series and led to 42 more. And bonus, I rewrote one of the four novels I'd set aside. *Time Lottery* won a Christy Award, proving that God can make new what we've tossed aside.

The best piece of writing advice I ever received was "Be willing to edit." While editing *The Invitation* I had to cut out 40,000 words! I'd written it with no clue about proper word count. It was a great exercise in learning how to tighten my writing. I even removed multiple characters who didn't add much to the story. Remember your book is *not* the Bible. It needs editing. My books still need editing. Always will.

Nancy Moser

www.nancymoser.com
Forty-five published books

Chapter 30

Kerry Nietz

It was supposed to be my last novel.

In the fall of 2003, my first book—a memoire entitled *Fox Tales: Behind the Scenes at Fox Software*—was published, and I hoped it would smooth the road for me to become a published novelist. Anyone familiar with the publishing business knows that few first books (or second books, or third books) breakout enough for a writer to have publishers knocking on their door. Few books, in fact, sell more than a couple hundred copies. But alas, I was naïve and optimistic.

Over the course of the next five years, I wrote a handful of potential novels, corrected them, and queried publishers about them. I had a few nibbles, but ultimately nothing happened. I'd written a lot of words, but none of them were going anywhere.

By the winter of 2007, I'd reached the conclusion that my dream of being a novelist wasn't going to happen. I'd tried a lot, learned a lot, but the "smooth road" now looked like an unplowed field.

Still, I had this idea about a computer programmer of the future bouncing around in my head. I also wanted to experiment with writing an entire novel in first person present tense. I'd written the prologue of *FoxTales* that way and wondered whether I could maintain that point of view for an entire novel.

I decided I'd write one last story . . . for me. I didn't care if anyone ever read it. I didn't care if I even corrected it or queried about it. I was simply going to write it for my own enjoyment. Then quit.

So, while sitting in an airport one day, I pulled out my laptop, created a new document, and wrote:

It is hard to describe, this buzzing in my head. It wakes me, obviously. But it is hard to clarify for someone like you —at least the type of person I assume you to be—someone with a free head.

Almost fifty thousand words later, I had a first draft. I read it over. It wasn't perfect and it was a little short. Yet there was something about the story, tentatively titled *2000 AP*, that I thought was truly unique. I decided to find a second opinion.

I knew of a guy, Jeff Gerke, who had started his own publishing house for speculative fiction. I knew he also worked as a freelance editor. One of his editorial services was a complete read through of a manuscript along with an opinion as to whether it was publishable. I hired him to perform that service with *2000 AP* in the spring of 2008.

Months went by.

Finally, in the fall of that same year he sent me a message: "I'm reading it now. I love it."

He concluded that the book needed a better beginning, a revised ending, and a handful of other changes. "If it had all those things," he said, "I would publish it myself."

I spent the better part of a year making those additions, and in the fall of 2009 the book, now titled *A Star Curiously Singing* was published. My first last novel. There have been over a dozen last novels since.

Kerry Nietz
http://www.nietz.com

Chapter 31

John Otte

One of the best and most impactful pieces of advice I ever received was an off-hand comment by Colleen Coble. It's one of my favorite stories to tell at a homeschool writers' workshop I teach at every summer. And I'm going to share the whole story now, so if you're not interested, you can skip to the end or just delete. I have no way of knowing. LOL!

So back in my early twenties, I was captivated by an idea for an epic sci-fi story. I wrote this tale and it turned out to be something like 250,000 words long, which took me several years to write. My genius idea was to break up this mammoth book into three parts and try to sell it as a trilogy. I edited the first book as best as I could (read: not very well) and then found out about the ACFW Conference. So I headed off to my first writing conference ever, absolutely convinced that I was going to come away with, if not a publishing contract and/or an agent, I'd have taken the first major steps toward getting one.

My pitch sessions were disastrous. The first, with Dave

Long of Bethany House, went well enough until I said the word "aliens." The moment I did that, his eyes glazed over and when I asked why, he said that they didn't publish those sorts of books anymore. I pointed out that Bethany had published Kathy Tyers and Karen Hancock, and he replied that the guy who acquired those two (namely Steve Laube) wasn't with the company anymore. After asking him to see if my proposal had been formatted correctly (the only question I could think to ask), I cut the session short and fled.

The next session was with Steve Laube. He listened to my idea and said, "I love it! Here's why you'll never sell it." He then pointed out each editor in the room and told me that none of the houses would ever touch a story like mine.

Feeling rather despondent, I was ready to give up writing altogether. Thankfully, that's when I had a mentor session with Deb Raney and Colleen Coble. They both listened to my bizarre idea politely (although I think Deb looked a bit shellshocked as I explained everything). They were encouraging about my rudimentary craft and encouraged me to keep going.

Rather than quit, I went home with renewed zeal for my story and spent the next two years, first tinkering with it and then rewriting the first book from the ground up. At the end of the two years, I decided to go back to ACFW and try again. I figured that this time, I would make some progress.

As it turned out, ACFW was in Minneapolis that year and since that was practically my backyard at the time, I volunteered to help. They assigned me to transporting faculty and other VIPs from the airport to the hotel. One of the people I was assigned to transport was Colleen. I was so thrilled to see her again! When I picked her up, I babbled at her about how she had been so encouraging and I thanked her.

She smiled graciously and then asked, "What are you pitching this year?"

"The same story I pitched two years ago!"

She gave me a worried look and asked if she could give me some advice. I said sure. She said she thought I should stop.

I was a bit confused. We were driving on the freeway. I suppose I could have pulled over . . .

She clarified that she thought I should maybe stop working on that book. She said that writers can often get locked in on one story they love and obsessively tinker with it for years, but it never goes anywhere. The best thing I could probably do was set aside that story and write a new one. Then I would grow and learn and improve my craft.

Once again, I was devastated at the thought. This was the story of my heart, the one I had dedicated so many years to. I went into the conference determined to prove that it was worth it.

I got nowhere with it.

So when I went home, I grudgingly decided to take Colleen's advice. I set aside the trilogy and wrote a different book. And then another one after that. And then another one after that.

That last book turned out to be my debut novel, *Failstate*, which finaled for the Christys the year it was published. And the book before that? That was *Numb*, another Christy finalist.

I haven't touched that epic sci-fi trilogy in over ten years. I now recognize just how broken its structure is and I still can't figure out if I could ever make it work. But I'm okay with that, because there are plenty of stories left for me to tell.

JOHN OTTE

https://www.amazon.com/stores/au-
thor/B008E99A7I/

Chapter 32

Carrie Stuart Parks

It's Christmas, 2003. Every year, my girlfriend and I would get each other presents. Nothing big—just some thoughtful trinket. I'd look for a tube of unusual-colored watercolor paint, a grape-shaped broach, or a small enameled box for her dresser. She'd find a Wizard of Oz ornament, Wicked Witch door stop, or Toto mug. Let's face it, I was easy. She was the hard one. She was very wealthy and could easily purchase anything she wanted. It would usually take me a full year of combing craft shows, antique shops, and art catalogs to find something.

This year I failed. We were a month out and I hadn't had a single inspirational bauble to give. I decided to write a short story about two women—one a fat, sassy forensic artist (I'm so original) and the other her beautiful friend. They go off on an adventure. The story ended up being over a hundred pages—a massive endeavor on my part. I didn't think I had that many words in me. I wrapped it and put it under her tree.

She called after the holidays and told me she loved the

story. I told her I loved the Wizard of Oz gift. Our lives moved on.

January turned to February of 2004. I was hard at work filling out the entries for the art booths I planned for the coming summer when I got a call from my friend's husband. He wanted to come over and talk to us. I was more than willing to pause my tedious task.

He arrived, saw what I was doing, and told me to stop. He said his wife had read him my story and that it had promise. He said I needed to move beyond the art and craft fairs, teaching forensic art, and my watercolor paintings and learn to write. And he would teach me.

My girlfriend was Barb Peretti, wife of Frank Peretti. The New York Times best-selling author offered to mentor me on how to write fiction. He would "teach me to fish."

I agreed.

I'd like to say all went swimmingly after that. My path was paved with success. Publishers would beat down my door to read the mesmerizing prose I'd weave.

But writing is hard and life is harder.

Less than a month after Frank made that offer, I was diagnosed with stage two breast cancer. I'd already been caring for my widowed mom, dying of end-stage emphysema. That spring, through the summer, and into the fall, between surgeries and chemo, I'd go to the Peretti home two days a week. I'd have two copies of my manuscript, a handful of highlighters, tabs, and pens, and sit across the kitchen table from Frank. While Barb plied us with cookies and expressos, I'd read what I'd written previously. I'd then wait breathlessly for his reaction. It was seldom good. Frank can make a lot of expressions illustrating what an overflowing toilet smelled like. On occasion, he'd nod or put a smiley face on the page.

I lived for those smiley faces.

I was now completely bald, without an income, and my mom was slipping away. My husband did what he could, including shaving his head, but he couldn't care for Mom, teach my classes, or do my art. We'd been a team, but our team was decimated.

I was learning to trust in God.

Along the way I learned persistence, determination, and quite frankly, endurance.

As I wrote, I became convinced I was the next Hemingway or Steinbeck. How could I lose? After all, I'd been excellent in English in high school, had a great imagination, and best of all, had Frank Peretti as a mentor. I started to look for an agent. I'd now been writing for four months so it was time.

I should have remembered Proverbs 16:18. "Pride goeth before destruction, and an haughty spirit before a fall." The agent I queried read my manuscript, called, and tore me a new one. She told me everything wrong with it. Trying to stifle my sobs, I asked if she would never consider me as a client because I wasn't good enough. She said, "Yes, but I just want you to write better."

By that fall, chemo over, mom worse, I continued to write. My hair returned. I wrote. My mom died. I wrote through my tears. We bought, remodeled, and moved into her house. I wrote through the paint and drywall. I punched away at that manuscript, my learning curve, for five more years.

Frank was always there, always teaching, and the smiley faces occurred more often.

It was now the summer of 2009 and I found an agent. I was so grateful that someone, *anyone*, wanted to represent me that I overlooked a lot of warning signs. She worked with me through the fall and spring on cleaning up the work, then sent it off to fourteen publishers.

Fourteen rejections.

Apparently, I really *wasn't* the next J. K. Rowling.

When my agent came back and gave me the news, she asked me if I wanted to go to smaller publishing houses. I said no. I was sick of this story and I had another idea for a book. I wanted this project put on the back burner. Maybe even toast it on that back burner.

Some of the lessons I'd learned by now had taken root. I wanted to continue to learn, to be a sponge to this craft. I'd consumed over eighty books on writing, attended ten writing conferences, and wrote copious notes in overflowing notebooks. I didn't want to be published for publishing's sake. I didn't want to self-publish. I wanted to write better. I wanted to have publishers fighting for my work.

By the fall of 2011, my agent dropped me. Without going into detail, let's just say I learned a lot from her, but it was an answer to prayer. By now I'd been working on the craft for seven years. I'd set aside the original book and started a new one. By January of 2013, I got a new agent. Less than a month later, he sent off a proposal to seven publishing houses with the second book. Twenty-eight minutes later, the first publishing house responded with a request for a full manuscript. Within a week, five of the seven publishers had expressed interest.

The book, A Cry From the Dust, quickly went to auction between two of the big five publishing houses for a three-book deal. It went on to final in the Christy Awards and won the Carol Award for best mystery-suspense-thriller.

The second book, The Bones Will Speak, was a rewrite of the original manuscript. It was an INSPY winner, Christy Award Finalist, Christian Retailing Best Finalist, and Family Fiction Readers Choice of the 15 Best Books of 2015. The subsequent books have done as well with awards.

I've continued to write, paint, and teach. In my "spare" time I'm an AKC dog show judge. God has been faithful and I'm blessed beyond belief for the cherished friendships I've discovered in the writing world.

In my bumpy, ten-year journey to publication, I've learned a lot and the teacher in me means I want to share those lessons. The best writing advice I've ever received or learned is:

Keep a teachable spirit. You can always grow, learn, and improve.

Trust God to have your back. He will always be with you, even during the darkest times.

Don't give up. Most people think they can write. Few can. Fewer still will see it through to the completion of that manuscript.

Keep pushing yourself. Don't settle for the first opportunity or easiest answer.

Help others along the way. We all start out pretty much in the same place. There will always be those further along in this craft than you and many more struggling behind you. Be like Frank and teach others to fish.

Stay humble. God likes to remind me of this rather often.

Blessings,

Carrie Stuart Parks

https://stuartparks.com/carrie-stuart-parks-home-page/

Five nonfiction drawing and watercolor books

Nine novels

Chapter 33

Trish Perry

When I went back to college for my Psychology degree, several professors encouraged me to consider writing. I loved that idea. I added Creative Writing classes to my course studies and wrote poems, journals, and short stories until I felt ready for a novel.

A writing professor advised me to write the kind of novel I enjoyed reading. Good advice. Although I was a strong Christian by that point, I thought back to a novel that had really pulled me in when I was much younger (and unsaved). It was called *Green Darkness*, and it involved a woman who experienced romantic love in 1968 but also in 16th Century England. I wish I could say it was a fantasy tale of time travel. But it was a well-told tale of a woman who had lived in two different times. As in reincarnated. Eesh.

Now that I was a Christian and knew better, it bothered me to consider that there were many impressionable readers out there who could be similarly drawn in by a good storyteller who espoused the "many lives" theology. I felt led to write what I thought would be a compelling story about a protagonist who is not a believer at first, who gets drawn into researching a "past life," and who comes dangerously close to a supernatural, spiritual catastrophe before realizing her desperate need for Christ. I had read and loved Frank Peretti's *This Present Darkness* and *Piercing the Darkness*. I knew it was possible to write a gripping spiritual warfare novel—I set out to do that.

It was a tricky undertaking. I was unpublished, and no one knew me as a Christian novelist. It was important that no reader misunderstand and think I was some New Age whacko. The supernatural aspect had to play a role in the book in order for the protagonist to continue thinking her "past life" was real. Through workshopping and generous mentoring from established Christian authors, I managed to write a novel that took my foolish protagonist to the spiritual edge and back again, into the loving arms of her Savior.

As so many first-time novelists do, I worked on that first novel for about five years. My heroine's supposed prior life was set during the Civil War. I researched my little heart out for the historical elements of the novel, as well as for the theological aspect that debunked the theory of reincarnation. I loved the work, but it was a *lot* of work.

When I finally got a chance to talk with prospective agents, I found my hopes quickly dashed. Spiritual warfare was no longer popular in Christian publishing. The publishing houses at conferences stipulated the genres they wanted. Nearly all of them listed "no spiritual warfare," as if they *knew* I was going to come sniffing around.

But something else happened near the end of that five-year process. The heaviness of my novel's subject matter was palpable. I still wanted to write, but I needed lightness.

Fun. Laughter. I had incorporated romance and a little humor in that first novel, but now I was moved to write a romantic comedy, still allowing for conflict and tension, but aiming for an upbeat journey for myself, my characters, and the reader.

I entered the first three chapters of the new manuscript in a writing contest. One of the judges was an agent who previously told me to cool it on the spiritual warfare novels. She didn't know who had written the new chapters, but she asked the group running the contest to have me call her. "This is exactly the kind of thing I represent."

That sentence couldn't have excited me more had it been set to music.

My new agent pushed me to hurry and finish the novel, *Too Good to Be True,* which she pitched to all of the big Christian houses while I got to work on a sequel. Harvest House Publishers bought the book but asked me what else I had. I had six new chapters written, which they asked for. Then they asked me to rewrite both books so that the sequel, *The Guy I'm Not Dating,* would come first, and *Too Good to Be True* would become the sequel. They also asked me to rewrite *Too Good to Be True* in third person, so the point of view would fit that of *The Guy I'm Not Dating.* Publishing will teach you flexibility, if nothing else!

So, my first novel was never published. My second novel was not my first release. My third novel was my first release.

Besides the importance of flexibility, I'd say the best writing advice I ever received was to read your book out loud. You'll hear the awkward parts. Your dialog *and* your narration will take on a conversational tone. That, after all, is what your novel is—a story you're telling your friend, the reader.

Trish Perry
TrishPerry.com
Thirty-six published books

Chapter 34

Deborah Raney

Before I can tell the story of how my first book was published, I first have to confess that I have been a quitter my whole life. Back when I first started thinking about finally writing *that* novel, my cupboards were full of unfinished scrapbooks, sewing projects, foreign language programs, and the ghosts of lessons and classes and decorating projects abandoned before completion.

So the fact that I'd wanted to write a book since I was a pre-teen was always shadowed by the knowledge that while I may start a book, whether or not I'd ever *finish* a book was questionable, indeed.

Add to that angst the fact that while I'd known for almost three decades that I wanted to write a novel, I did not have even one idea in mind. Still, the dream of writing "the great American novel" wouldn't let go of me.

In 1990, when our older three children were fourteen, ten, and eight, God blessed us with an "oops baby." As our little #4 became a toddler, the time crept closer and closer for our oldest son to go to college. We didn't have a penny saved toward that end (because I'd gotten to live my dream of being a stay-at-home mom), and I wondered if writing that novel might be just the ticket to allow me to make some money writing from home while still being there with our baby.

How naive I was to think that writing a novel might actually pay for any significant portion of a college education. Ah, but don't ever underestimate God!

Sitting around the supper table one cold night in December of 1993, the conversation turned to a family we knew where the wife had been diagnosed with early-onset Alzheimer's Disease. Our kids' perspectives were fascinating, and that night I lay wide awake in bed as a story about a family dealing with the wife and mother's diagnosis of Alzheimer's formed in my imagination.

Still, there was that nagging fear that I would be a quitter in this, but I'd heard somewhere that if you wrote just one page a day, at the end of a year, you'd have 365 pages, and that is a book. Surely, I could do that, couldn't I?

On New Year's Day 1994, I sat down with a red felt tip pen and a spiral steno pad and wrote what became the prologue for *A Vow to Cherish.* I typed my budding manuscript up on my state-of-the-art electric typewriter, carefully fixing any typos with Wite-Out. (I know, I know . . . I'm showing my age.)

I handed the pages to my husband and asked for his honest opinion. Expressionless, standing in the kitchen of the little duplex where we raised our kids, he read it. And then he handed the pages back to me, sounding a little incredulous. "Honey, this is *good.* Keep writing."

I did. Every day after the kids were in school and the baby was down for her nap or playing happily on her own (thank you, Lord, for an easy baby!) I would write as many pages as I could. When Ken saw that I was serious about this writing thing, my sweet husband brought home an "obsolete" computer that his workplace sold cheap in an auction. He taught me to use it and from that point, there was no stopping me!

The story poured from me like no story has since, and by the end of May of that year, I had a 70,000-word manuscript ready to send off to publishers. By then, Ken had two children's picture books published, and I knew from his experience that rejection was part of the life of an author. So I sent out twenty copies of the manuscript—and waited. Sure enough, the rejections came rolling in.

Most of them said, "People don't want to read a story about illness." But that wasn't what my story was about! Couldn't they see that it was about so much more? Well, no, they probably couldn't. Mostly because I had *told* the bulk of my story instead of *showing* it.

But in September, I received an offer from Avalon Press in New York. And a couple weeks later, I had another offer from Harold Shaw Publishers, which a few years later became an imprint of Random House's WaterBrook Press.

In November of 1994, President Ronald Reagan announced in a letter to the nation that he was suffering from Alzheimer's Disease. Suddenly this awful disease was in the headlines, and there seemed to be a corresponding interest in my novel.

Ultimately, I was offered contracts from three different publishers, but the first two, while well-respected companies, were only offering me an advance of $1500 and a print run of 1500 copies. Math is not my strong suit, but I could calculate that this was a drop in the bucket compared to what we'd just been told our son's four-year education would cost.

Even so, I was thrilled that someone wanted to publish my manuscript. While I was trying to decide which of those two publishers to sign with (one was secular, one Christian), another publisher stepped in. And without even waiting to hear what kind of contract they were offering, I said yes.

Because, you see, that publisher was Bethany House. They had been my first choice and the first place I sent my manuscript. Because they published Janette Oke's novels, which had been so incredibly inspirational to me as I became a wife and mom. And also because I loved the covers they created for their books.

I began working with my editor, dear Sharon Asmus (who is in heaven now), and she so graciously taught me how much I did *not* know about writing: POV? What was that? Show-don't-tell? I don't understand! Pacing? I thought that was something you did when you were bored. Oh, there was so much to learn, but I loved the process of editing (still do to this day) and I could see how much better my story was getting under Sharon's deft guidance.

One day, about two weeks into the editing process, Sharon called to tell me that they had my contract ready to send out but that they wanted to go over the details before they mailed the paperwork. When she told me the amount they would be paying as an advance on royalties, and then revealed that they were offering me a *two*-book contract, I had to sit down. For the total amount was—to the penny—what our son's four years of room, board, and tuition would cost! (Remember, this was almost thirty years ago and college was much more affordable then!) Nevertheless, I still consider it a miracle and a blessing from God.

My first novel went on to be the inspiration for World Wide Pictures's award-winning film of the same title, launching my career as a writer. It was heady stuff for this little Kansas farm girl to get to go to Hollywood to the premiere of *A Vow to Cherish*!

For many years, every penny I made in royalties went to some college. It was a happy, happy day when our youngest graduated. But I would be remiss not to mention that my experience with getting my first book published is not typical. And with the forty-plus books I've had published since, there have been some low lows along with the high highs.

Still, whenever I lament the hard parts of being a writer—the long days with butt-in-chair, the pressure of deadlines, the disappointing sales, the canceled contracts, the rejections (yes, established authors still get rejections)—my writing critique partner, my dear friend Tamera Alexander, will ask the million dollar question. "So what would you *rather* do than be a writer?"

It's a fair question, and I can answer with all my heart: "Not one thing. I love being a writer, and I know that's exactly what God has called and gifted me to do."

The best piece of writing advice I ever got? Read your manuscript aloud, especially the dialogue sections. I'm always amazed how many mistakes I find when I read aloud. More importantly, I often change the dialogue after reading aloud because I realize I didn't have the inflection quite right or that there's a quicker or better way to get the idea across. If your book might become an audiobook, it's all the more important to read your work aloud to be sure everything sounds as great in spoken form as it does in writing.

DEBORAH RANEY

www.deborahraney.com

Forty plus books and counting

Chapter 35

Gayle Roper

I *think I'll try a novel.* I'd written a short story and had it published. Why not a novel? I was a young mom at home with two little boys, and I wanted a mental challenge. I'd always read as if my life depended on it, so writing a story seemed a logical thing to me.

I knew nothing about publishing except I needed a publisher. I was writing a mystery, and I'd read mysteries Moody Press published. I decided to send my mystery there. When I finished three chapters, I sent them to Chicago.

Some nice lady sent me a letter saying they'd like to see the rest of the book. I was excited at the prospect of having a book with my name on the spine, so every time I finished a chapter, I sent it off to this nice lady. She very kindly kept the chapters until there was a whole novel on her desk.

Yes, you read that correctly. I submitted my first novel chapter by chapter. What you need to understand is that I was writing this book in the late 1960's. I didn't know there was a prescribed way to do things, and if there were resources out there to tell me how, I knew nothing of them.

Moody published *Fear Haunts the Summer* in 1970. It did like most first novels which is to say very poorly. It was remaindered to a mission to seamen in the Orient. Know any sailors who would have wanted to read a book with a screaming woman on the cover? On a positive note, I was able to reuse some of the plot points from this less than stellar seller in *Summer Shadows*, which I wrote thirty years later. This book was a Christy and RITA finalist.

Since *Fear Haunts the Summer,* I've published 60+ books and won numerous awards including the RITA Award and the Carol Award as well as two Lifetime Achievement Awards. I owe my fifty-year career to that kind lady in Chicago.

The best piece of writing advice I ever received was adapt and persevere. No industry stays static. Be aware but remain true to yourself and the calling God has put on your life.

GAYLE ROPER

www.gayleroper.com

Sixty plus titles

Chapter 36

James L. Rubart

One semi-sunny day in the spring of 2000, my wife announced she was going on a fast.

"Why?"

"I don't know."

"How long?"

"Till I get the answer."

"What's the question?"

"No clue."

At the end of 24 hours, I asked how she was doing and if she'd gotten the answer.

"Starving. And no."

At the end of 48 hours I asked again. Same response. Halfway through day three, as we drove home in our Jeep, a light bulb exploded over my head. I felt the Spirit say, "I've given you the ability and passion to become a novelist. When are you going to step into your destiny?"

I turned to my wife and said, "I know why you're fasting."

"Why?"

"I'm supposed to be a novelist!"

She turns to me and says, "Wait a minute. I'm hungry for three days and *you* get the answer?"

(It was a pretty funny moment.)

Five years later, in the fall of '05, I finished my first novel. Total word count: 148,000. (I had no idea what I was doing.) I sent a query letter to four agents. Three of them rejected me immediately. The fourth asked if the manuscript was finished and how long.

I of course thought, "This is it! I'm going to be published!"

When I responded it was finished and clocked in at 148,000 words, he wrote back with a scathing e-mail that ended with, "THIS IS OUR LAST COMMUNICATON!" It took me out. I stopped working on the novel. I stopped querying people. I stopped reading fiction. Buh-bye dream I'd had since 7th grade.

But of course God was not so easily discouraged. A few months later, In the spring of '06, a friend invited me to go with him to the Mount Herman Christian writing conference. I didn't want to go. At all. I was done. But my wife said, "You need to go. I feel like the Spirit is saying you absolutely have to be there." I went, and by the end of the conference there were five editors and three agents interested in my manuscript.

In early August of that year, I went to a writing clinic with Cec Murphy who helped take my writing to a new level and I applied those lessons to my manuscript. By the end of August, I had an agent. My agent shopped that first novel to all the major houses in the fall of '06. The general consensus from the publishers was, "This guy can write, we just don't know what to do with this kind of novel." Yeah, it was a bit out there. Here's the log line for the story, you be the judge:

A young Seattle software executive inherits a home down on the Oregon coast that turns out to be physical manifestation of his soul.

But one editor said, "I was so impressed with Rubart's material, I found myself wishing another author had written it." In other words, an author with a name. He just couldn't take a chance on a newbie.

So I started writing my second novel. But again, God had other plans.

Fast forward to a year later, fall of 2007. I was at the annual ACFW writing conference and had set up an appointment with the above editor (David Webb) to pitch him my new novel, *Book of Days.*

When I walked in the room, I didn't say hello. I simply sat down and read his own e-mail back to him. (It's the marketing guy in me.) David got a smile on his face and said, "So you're the guy who wrote *Rooms.*" I smiled back and nodded yes.

David said "I've read over 200 manuscripts since I read yours and yours is the one I can't get out of my head. Do you want to take another run at it?"

"YES!!!!!" Don't worry, that was only in my mind. I'm sure I was much cooler than that on the outside. Well, kind of sure.

David took it to pub board on Monday, May 4th, 2008. I asked my agent how long it would take to get an answer. He said we'd probably get an answer on the afternoon of the 4th but it could be a few days later. Monday afternoon came and went with no answer. Tuesday came and went. Wednesday came and went. Thursday and Friday came and went.

On Tuesday of the following week I emailed my agent. No answer yes or no. No communication at all from David. Another week went by without word. After three weeks with no answer I was praying about it and felt like the

Spirit said "You'll only be able to experience this kind of anticipation once. So enjoy it. You're going to get the contract."

At that point I was at total peace and enjoyed the anticipation much like when I was a kid in the days before Christmas. On June 28th we got a deal point memo.

Rooms came out a little less than two years later, in early April 2010. It hit the bestseller list and won RT Book Review's Inspirational Novel of the Year. And better than that, I've received hundreds of emails from readers telling me how the story changed their life.

So I'm one of those who doesn't have a novel in the drawer, and you're probably asking, "What in the world would Jim have done without his wife?"

Exactly.

The best piece of writing advice I've ever received: "Get a pair of high-end track shoes. Put them on. Take one last look at the publishing industry, then turn and run in the opposite direction as fast as you can. If you're simply unable to do that, you have a real shot at becoming an author."

James L. Rubart

Jameslrubart.com

Books published: Ten solo, six co-authored.

Chapter 37

Jill Eileen Smith

I began my first novel on the life of King David at the tail end of the 1980s. I'd co-taught a Bible study on his life and didn't want it to end. I wanted to read a story that would take me *there.* Thus began my search for a novel that would satisfy me.

When I couldn't find one, I sat down to write the book I wanted to read. The trouble was, I didn't know a thing about writing a book of any kind, much less a novel. But I had the Bible as a guide, and David's life has a lot of good plot points, so I learned as I went.

A two-volume epic tale later, I wrote "the end" on a book that had somehow turned from the book I wanted to read to the book I wanted to see published. I had no experience or connections to the publishing world, though I had begun to research how to go about seeing that happen.

After twenty-eight rejections, I tucked that book into two boxes under the bed. On the bright side, I did have one publisher ask to read the whole thing. I had another editor ask me to write the story of David's first wife, Michal, because her publishing house, Harper San Francisco, didn't take stories about male lead characters for biblical fiction.

I naively turned her down because I couldn't see a happy ending to Michal's story. I proposed a story about Hannah instead, but unfortunately, Harper had decided to close its biblical fiction line. I would find as time went on that I tended to be a day late and a dollar short . . . sorry for the cliché . . . but I was always trying to break in when what I wanted to write was no longer popular.

So, I joined a local critique group and found an online writer support group where I met Brandilyn Collins who invited me to join ACRW, which is now ACFW. I even got my first agent for that first conference, but I still didn't know what I was doing. And I felt like I was way out of my element.

But through ACFW, I ended up trying two other critique groups. One of those groups helped me to become publishable, not to mention I made some great friends there. While in that group, my first book finally sold. Of course, I was the last of us to sell . . . but that's just the way things go sometimes.

What happened to that first two-volume epic of King David?

A few years after that editor at Harper suggested I write about Michal, I took her up on her suggestion. I wrote and rewrote that book until I couldn't work on it any more. I set it aside and worked on a book about Abigail. I spent five years writing Abigail's story while I home-schooled my sons. I learned point of view during those five years. You can probably tell by now that I learned writing the hard way.

After five years, Abigail garnered interest from one publisher, but again, no thanks. So, I wrote in other genres —romantic suspense, a time-travel novel, women's fiction, and more. I had three agents, the last of which I'm still with today—Wendy Lawton. She loved *Michal,* which I still wanted to sell. I had turned that two-volume epic on King David's life into The Wives of King David series.

But my first two agents had already shopped *Michal,* the first book in that would-be series, all over the Christian market. Wendy told me that she was going to have to shelve the project because it had been around the CBA block too many times. She focused on selling one of my suspense novels instead.

That was in the spring of 2007. I'd been writing for twenty years by then, and had come to the very end of my hope of ever seeing a book in print.

I spend a lot of time journal praying, so one day, after Wendy told me she had to shelve *Michal,* I wrote a prayer to the Lord. In that prayer, I gave Wendy one year to sell something. *Anything.* It was not an ultimatum prayer, and Wendy knew nothing about it. I just wanted God to show me that if I'd misread Him and He had something else for me to do, then to please tell me. I couldn't take any more rejection. I dated the entry and closed the journal. Then I promptly forgot about my prayer.

A few months later, when I knew that Wendy was at ICRS shopping my suspense, I had what I call a "fantasy prayer". It wasn't a prayer in any real sense. Just a pipe dream. But in that "dream," I imagined an editor asking Wendy if she had any biblical fiction. The story of David's wives had become the stories of my heart, and I couldn't quite let them go.

That summer my boys were making a music video for a local musician. I provided the food for the crew, so I had to run home to get the food. While I was there, I checked my computer's email. This was before the days of smart phones where I could have found the information there. I noticed an email from Wendy. Did she have the latest version of *Michal?* While she was at the Oregon Christian Writer's Conference, she sat next to an editor who told her she was looking for a work of biblical fiction. (My fantasy not-really-a-prayer come true!) Wendy told her, "Have I got the book for you!"

Talk about shaking all over! I quickly checked to be sure she had the latest version of the book, then rushed back to the set of the video shoot.

Of course, publishing is all about hurry up and wait, and a few months passed while I waited and tried to not bite my nails every day. But the truth was, I was nervous. I'd been turned down so many times. Rejection makes the heart ache. But the lessons I'd learned while waiting had also taught me that I needed to surrender this all to the Lord.

So, while Amy Grant's "Sweet Will of God" played over the speakers as I sat in my car in the garage, I bent over the steering wheel and surrendered it all to God. This desire had to be His will or I didn't want it. I went into the house at peace.

I'm not sure how soon after that surrender that I got "the call," but it happened one Saturday morning—yes, a Saturday! Wendy called me to tell me the publisher wanted The Wives of King David series of three books. It still had to go to the president for his signature, so we didn't have the contract yet, but the offer was there. Back to waiting a little longer, but wow! I couldn't believe it had actually happened!

And the biggest surprise, saving the best for last, was that the editor who acquired The Wives of King David for Revell, was the same editor who had suggested I write about Michal when she worked at Harper San Francisco.

Sixteen years later, we were working together on the book she had suggested that I'd turned down.

Lonnie Hull DuPont was that editor, and she remained my editor until her retirement. She acquired twenty-two books from me, all of those that are now in print or e-book format, as well as, the one releasing in 2024. She didn't edit all of them as she retired before they were written, but I owe her my career. She took a chance on biblical fiction and on me when the only people who could write it were already well-established authors. And by her taking that chance, the door opened for more writers of this genre to break into traditional publishing.

In December of 2007, I happened to find that journal prayer from the spring of that year. I read it in awe of what God had done. In six months, He had answered my prayer. I had the confirmation that I had not misread His plans for me. Honestly, it was a relief because I hadn't trained to do anything else except teach piano to beginners, and I didn't love that job. Writing had always been my passion, even if I simply wrote my prayers to God. But He took that desire far beyond what I could have ever imagined.

We never know what God will do with our first attempt at novel writing. My very first two-volume epic has now been happily shredded. It did not deserve to see the light of day. But I learned so much because of those years of study and working on a book I thought only I would want to read.

I wanted to quit so many times, but God also put people into my life who encouraged me. One was the late B.J. Hoff who wrote the most encouraging emails. The best writing advice I ever received came from her when she famously said, "It matters not if the world has heard or approves or understands . . . the only applause we're meant to seek is that of nail-scarred hands."

Whenever we write, even if our motives aren't quite what they should be when we begin, we would do well to remember her words. We might write a book, many books, such as those that still sit on my computer that the world will never read. And that's okay. We're not meant to seek the approval of people. Write what God places on your heart to write. Don't write what you know. You can always learn what you don't know. Write what you love for the glory of God.

And when you finish that first manuscript, start the next. You might never publish that first book. But if God called you to write, don't give up until He tells you to.

The Wives of King David went on to be my bestselling books. Only God could have seen what took twenty years to come to pass.

Jill Eileen Smith
www.jilleileensmith.com
Nineteen books and four novellas

Chapter 38

Carla Stewart

I can't remember when I didn't dream of being a writer, penning books like those I'd devoured from childhood on. A pipe dream, my daddy would've said. In my teens, I tucked away the desire and chose the more practical path. I became a nurse, and along the way married my college sweetheart, had four boys, and a busy, fulfilling life. Still, with each novel I read, the dream lingered. One day. Someday, I'll become a writer.

In the blink of an eye, I was fifty years old. The old dream reared its head and occupied my thoughts day and night. Several things happened that year, though, that spurred me on. I was in a job that wasn't a good fit for me, but with college kids and one teen still at home, we needed the extra money and the insurance my job provided. Also, my mother had terminal cancer, and it hit me. Time was fleeting, and if I were to ever write the novel I dreamed about, I'd better get started.

After prayerful consideration, I quit my job and devoted the last months of my mom's life to her. God provided a new job for my husband (with benefits!) so all I had to do was write. Whoa! I soon learned that I knew nothing about writing an entire book or the writing world.

Off to the bookstore I went and purchased a couple of books on writing. Excitement I hadn't felt in a long time coursed through my veins as I huddled over the computer and wrote the first word. The first sentence. A whole paragraph. I took a notebook to my youngest son's baseball games and jotted down timelines, plot ideas, and crafted my cast of characters. And I didn't tell a soul. When I had around a hundred pages, I finally confessed to my husband what I was doing. He was delighted and became my cheerleader from that moment on.

The words and chapters poured out of me. Within three months my novel was complete. I discovered a writing group two hours from the rural area where we lived and was delighted that they had a conference coming up the next month. I signed up right away and arrived at the conference with the jitters and the feeling that I had no idea what I was doing. I didn't sign up for any appointments with editors or agents because I didn't even know you could do that.

In one of the general sessions, as we were waiting for the speaker to arrive, a gentleman seated behind me tapped me on the shoulder and asked what I wrote. I told him I'd just completed my first novel. He asked what it was about. I gave him the long answer. Again, I didn't know about pitch lines or being succinct. He nodded and smiled and introduced himself. My heart raced, and my mouth might have flown open. He was an editor with a major Christian publisher, and he had just asked to read my book. Not three chapters or a synopsis—the entire book! I was thrilled and pictured holding my first published book in my hands. Who knew it would be so easy?

I proofed my manuscript one last time and mailed it

off, knowing I was on the road to being a real author. Two months later, the manuscript came back to me.

"Thank you for letting me read your novel. I'm sorry . . ."

My throat closed off, and I was afraid to read on, but the letter filled the whole page—paragraphs of critique from this busy, professional editor who had not only read my book, but offered praise for the parts he liked and critique for the things that didn't work. And oh boy, there were lots of those.

He ended by saying that he enjoyed the story and wrote these words, "You have an engaging voice. Keep writing."

Happy, grateful tears filled my eyes. I wasn't a terrible writer. I just needed to stick with it and learn the ropes. I tucked the manuscript away and knew this probably wouldn't be my first published book, but there would be others. I went to more conferences, entered writing contests, published a few magazine articles, wrote for anthologies and literary journals. I also revisited that first manuscript a few times, and new ideas began to emerge. I worked on craft, got professional editorial opinions, and joined a critique group. *Keep writing.* The words from the rejection letter sustained me. That, and a lot of coffee. But eventually, almost ten years to the day after I quit my job, I held my first published novel in my hands. Had it not been for this gracious, thoughtful editor, I might very well have given up. Instead, I cherish being part of the writing community, treasure the friendships I've made, and adore the readers who've loved each of my novels.

It wasn't a pipe dream after all. And being a late blooming writer has been bigger than all my dreams. More than I could ever imagine.

Looking back over the last two decades, the best piece

of writing advice I received came in that first rejection letter. *You have an engaging voice. Keep writing.*

Carla Stewart
www.carlastewart.com
Six published novels

Chapter 39

Kathleen Y'Barbo-Turner

I started writing romance novels after my youngest child went off to preschool. By the time I found out that how-to-write books and writers groups existed, I had completed six complete novels. Author DiAnn Mills joined my local writers group, and we became friends. At the time, she had something like one or two books published, so of course I was in awe.

A few months later, I got a call from DiAnn asking if I knew anything about Texas Rangers because she was putting together a historical novella collection for Barbour Publishing and thought of including me. I said of course I did then hung up and started researching. The next day I sent her a synopsis for a story based on a true story from my mother's side of the family that I adapted to include a Texas Ranger as a love interest.

I was so green back then that I didn't realize a proper proposal needed chapters. Apparently it was fine because less than two weeks later, I got an email from Becky Germany at Barbour offering a contract for my novella, *Saving Grace*. That was 1999, and *Saving Grace* has been in several Barbour collections over the year. It's the only Barbour novella of mine that has never gone out of print.

I've written over 100 traditionally published novels, novellas, and nonfiction books, but that one is special.

Kathleen Y'Barbo-Turner
www.kathleenybarbo.com

Chapter 40

Dan Walsh

I knew I wanted to write novels way back in 11th grade, but life took me in a radically different direction when I came to Christ a year later. I experienced what is often referred to as a "call to ministry" and wound up becoming a full-time pastor at age twenty-eight. I figured maybe God would let me fulfill my writing dream when I retired. My love of fiction never waned, though, and I kept reading fiction novels the entire time I served as a pastor.

Fast-forward twenty-two years to 2007.

I had begun experiencing some serious burnout and attended a workshop on this at a pastor's conference. They suggested we needed to find something we really enjoyed, some hobby or pastime, that refreshed our batteries and told us to make time to do that in our schedule. On the way home, my wife reminded me how much I loved to write fiction back in high school and suggested I might try that.

I liked the idea and began to pray about an idea for a novel. It was near Christmas, and we always loved to watch the same movies every holiday, like *It's a Wonderful Life* and Dickens' *Christmas Carol.* After watching one of those, I found myself wishing I could somehow write a Christmas story that at least had the potential to affect people the way these classic tales affected me.

Over the next several days, this amazing idea for a Christmas story just started dropping into my head. I began to write it down. After a week or so, I basically had created the synopsis for what would later become my first published novel, *The Unfinished Gift.* During that holiday, I read the synopsis to my wife, and she absolutely loved it, said I should definitely start writing the book.

So, that's what I did in my spare time over the next 12 months. Reading chapters to her as I finished them. She really felt like I was creating something that could definitely be published. After completing the book, I knew it likely had flaws, so I bought a half-dozen "craft books" on writing at B&N. With their help, I began a six-month process of self-editing my work. I re-wrote the manuscript several times as a result of what I'd learned from those books.

Researching the internet on the steps necessary to get published in Christian Fiction, I quickly realized I needed to attract a good literary agent. That led to a process of learning how to write great query letters and a gripping synopsis. I made a list of what looked to me to be the Top fifteen literary agents in CF. I picked the first three, went on their websites, and mailed each of them a package based on their requirements.

Then I waited. I figured I'd start getting rejection letters after several weeks. After being rejected by the first three agents, I'd send stuff out to the next three on the list.

That's not what happened.

After a few weeks, I got one rejection letter. The other 2 agents contacted me, one by mail, the other by phone, saying they loved what I sent and wanted to read the rest of the book. The one who called me seemed far more eager, and after verifying that she really was an "A-list" agent, I agreed to sign on with her. Her name was Karen Solem with Spencerhill Associates.

She was able to land a great contract with Revell Publishing six weeks later. That began a relationship that resulted in a total of twelve published novels with them over the next six years. But it all started with that first book, *The Unfinished Gift*. The next holiday season (2009), it released wherever books are sold in hardback, paperback, and ebook (although back then ebooks were very new). My wife took a picture of me holding a hardback copy from an end cap at our local B&N.

The Unfinished Gift became a holiday bestseller, was nominated and won two Carol Awards (Best Debut Author and Best Historical Fiction) in 2010. It literally launched my writing career. I was able to "retire" from pastoring and have been writing full-time ever since. This past October, I just published my twenty-eighth novel, called *What's Best For Them*.

My Best Writing Advice: Probably comes from my favorite writing quote from the late Elmore Leonard – "*In your writing, try to leave out all the parts the readers skip*." He was known for writing page-turning novels, so I decided that would be my goal. My advice then would be to forget about learning how to do things like grow your platform, the latest and best online marketing techniques, and spend your time learning how to write novels people can't stop reading once they start. That's what people want, a great story well told. Write books like that, and you will do well.

Dan Walsh
www.danwalshbooks.com

Chapter 41

Beth White

I'm Beth White, author of sixteen full-length Christian romance novels and four novellas, published by Tyndale House, Zondervan, Love Inspired, and Revell. Tyndale published my first novella in one of the new HeartQuest Romance anthologies in December of 1999—a contemporary romantic suspense story entitled "Miracle on Beale Street."

But "Miracle" was not my first finished work. In the early '90's, when my children were small, I was a stay-at-home mom who helped make ends meet by teaching piano and voice lessons in my home. I was busy, but I've always been creative, and the itch to write fiction has never left me alone since I was a very young teenager. I can't even remember when I started a short story about a college-age romance between Christian music major Gina and bad boy drummer Dan, but at some point it grew into a full-length book that I actually finished. I had hand-written a lot of it in a spiral notebook, but eventually typed it up on a little electric typewriter (remember White-Out tape?).

I'm a voracious reader, and I thought *Gina's Song* was at

least as good as paperback books in the used bookstore I frequented—and it was different from what I saw in Christian bookstores, because it was frankly mainly about the love story. I was aware that Christian-worldview teen romances existed (*Christy Miller* by Robin Jones Gunn, for example), but I thought I had a unique twist that might be publishable.

What the heck, I thought. *Let's send this to a publisher and see what happens.*

I look back at my ignorant self and wonder at my own audacity, not to mention lack of understanding of the whole publication process. I had no idea how to find the address of a book publishing company, let alone an editor who might read an unsolicited manuscript (I didn't even really think about the fact that my manuscript would be unsolicited). I did have the sense to realize I'd have a better chance if I'd approach a company who produced stories remotely similar to mine. So I visited a Christian bookstore near my house and found the *Christy Miller* books.

Ah. Bethany House in Carol Stream, Illinois. Bingo!

Still, no street address. So I went to the library and found a giant reference volume that contained addresses of every publisher in America. And—how about this?—the addresses included the names of Acquisitions Editors. I had no idea what that meant, but I dutifully packaged up my manuscript in a brown envelope and mailed it off with a very awkward cover letter to editor Carol Johnson at Bethany House.

Then I went about my music-teacher-mommy business while I waited. And waited. And waited some more. Six months went by before I received a reply. "Dear Mrs. White, we are interested in your story, which has strong characters and an interesting plot. We had entertained the idea of launching a college-age Young Adult line of romances, but the submissions committee feel that the market is not strong enough to support the venture at this time. However, if you have another story idea in a more established genre, please feel free to send it to us."

I was crushed. And paralyzed. I had no other immediate ideas. I didn't even really know what that meant. I didn't realize that "We are interested in your story" and the fact that a committee had seriously considered it was high praise. All I saw was rejection. I mourned for several months, because from what I could tell, Bethany House was the only publisher appropriate for my type of story. And they didn't want it.

What I did next, however, was the best thing I could have done. I joined Romance Writers of America and met several other Christian writers, one of whom became a dear friend and critique partner. I began to learn that I *was* a good writer with a lot of potential, but I was very far from publishable. It was a miracle that I'd reached an editor at a reputable publishing house with a slush pile submission, let alone attracted a serious read. I soon realized that even if they'd bought my story, there would have had to be serious rewrites before it was worthy of the light of day. I went to local and national writing conferences, met multi published authors who were generous with their time and experience and instruction.

In the spring of 1998, I met Kathy Olson, an editor at Tyndale House, who read the first few pages of a second manuscript I'd started by then (which took several years to sell to a different publisher). Kathy encouraged me and eventually recommended that I submit a novella to Tyndale's new HeartQuest romance line. She facilitated a contract for the second novella I submitted, which became "Miracle on Beale Street."

What can I say about *Gina's Song*? It is buried somewhere in a file, I think on a floppy disk in my attic. I've worked on it a time or two since 1995, but it will never see publication. It is too broken. I've cannibalized many elements from it for other stories, so it's had its uses. It is a funny part of my publishing career story, and I think of it with fond sentiment. Just don't ask to look at it. Maybe after I'm dead somebody will unearth it and shudder with sympathy for the delusional young woman who submitted it cold-turkey to professionals at Bethany House.

Dear Lord, I hope not.

The best piece of writing advice I ever got was BE NICE to everybody and don't burn bridges.

Beth White (sometimes writing as Elizabeth White)
bethwhite.net
Twenty books to date

Chapter 42

Roseanna M. White

I always say that I've been writing stories from the moment my first-grade teacher taught me what a subject and verb were. Primary school was filled with brilliant (ahem) tales about magic hair bows, pink bunnies that lived in the clouds, and unicorns that controlled the weather with their magical horns. Everyone was a princess, and whatever age I was, that was the magic number all characters should be. I wrote countless short stories that I hand copied into little books and illustrated. I started countless tales that I intended to be chapter books but never quite finished.

Then in seventh grade, I decided it was time to stop messing around and get serious. I was going to write a "real" book. For adults. It was going to be historical romance (never mind that at age twelve I knew about nothing about romance beyond what I'd read or seen in Disney movies). It was going to be a "real" length. So I did what most young writers do—I blatantly knocked off my favorite historical romance, which at that point in time was *The Hawk and the Jewel* by Lori Wick.

Uninspired and unoriginal? Sure. But here's the thing —I wrote the book. It took me a year and half, but I wrote the book. It was scrawled on notebook paper, mostly during school, in a variety of pencil and pen and anything else I had handy. I used stick-on tabs to mark where chapters started. I frequently drew my ideas for the cover and shoved them in the three-ring binder I kept it in. When I needed a new character name, I would shout out the need to my classmates and let them make suggestions. I called this brilliant work of literature *Golden Sunset, Silver Tear* and was so, so proud when I finally finished it in my eighth-grade year.

The summer between middle school and high school, I sat down to type it all into the computer . . . and make it more mine and less Lori Wick's in the process. I had no idea what things like word count meant, but as it turns out, I did indeed have a full-length novel in my possession. And I'd learned something valuable about structure by mimicking Lori's beautiful work, then about revising and rewriting as I took out all the elements that were hers and replaced them with what was mine. Convinced I would be published by age sixteen, I bought a copy of *The Christian Writers Market Guide* and sent out my hard copy proposals and SASEs and prepared myself for the dream to come true.

Cue the steady stream of rejection letters. I'm talking form letters where there was literally a list of checkboxes of why my query was of no interest to them (I'm looking at you, Bethany House!). And then one, still a form letter, but with a handwritten note. I still remember what it said: "We can't publish this, but you clearly have talent. Keep writing!" Well, who was I to disobey some random editor?

I rewrote that book again in high school, while I was working on something totally different, which I finished before I graduated as well. I gave it another round in college, and then did a complete overhaul after I'd graduated with my bachelors, joined a writers organization, and realized that I knew very little about modern fiction writing after all. By that time, I'd finished nine other novels too. I'd learned a lot about the writing process, about writing rules, and about the industry. I'd submitted countless books to countless publishers. My husband and I had even started a small press and used one of my other books as the guinea pig.

By the time I attended my first writers conference, I decided that my latest version of *Golden Sunset, Silver Tear*, now entitled *Fire Eyes,* would be the book I pitched. I ended up signing with the agent I met with, and the editor—from Bethany House—I met ended up taking the book the committee. They ultimately passed on it, but those meetings are what really started me on the path to traditional publication. I ended up writing a book for Summerside/Guideposts, a series for Harvest House, and I had two successful books with our own company.

Then the *Downton Abbey* craze struck, and my agent (a different one, as that first one retired) emailed to say, "Hey, everyone's looking for something Edwardian. Do you have anything?"

I didn't. But I remembered that first historical romance. It had been Victorian, but . . . why not see if it would work in a new setting? I binge watched the first season of *Downton*, gave myself a crash course in All Things Edwardian, reread my old manuscript, and made a plan to give it another complete overhaul.

And magic happened. Things that never quite made sense suddenly became new twists, new characters, new insights. The heroine who never quite fit in Victorian times made *perfect* sense in the changing world of the Edwardian era. The mystery deepened, the characterizations followed suit, and focusing both on the upstairs and downstairs of English society made me grin in delight. I *loved* the way the story came together, and my agent loved it too. She loved it so much that she sent it off to a bunch of publishing houses, and one offered me a contract . . . until they realized I was still working on a series for Harvest House, and this would interfere. That fell through, but when my time at Harvest was complete, my agent said, "Let's submit that one again."

I knew, as that book made the rounds yet again, that this time it was going to find its home. And as I prayed about it, I also became increasingly certain that it was going to land at Bethany House . . . who had already looked at it and rejected it twice before in its previous versions. Imagine my surprise when I got an email from that BHP editor I'd met seven years before at my first writers conference, that said, "I recognize that story that just came across my desk! I can't wait to talk it about it at the committee! Love what you've done with it!"

She remembered! She remembered me, she remembered that story. And when Bethany House offered a contract for that series, she was the editor I got to work with on it.

By the time *The Lost Heiress* released in 2015, the manuscript was twenty years old. I had nine other books out from three different publishers. It had been completely rewritten four solid times, with countless tweaks in between. The setting changed, the main characters' families changed, and the title had changed innumerable times. But it was still that first story. The heart was still there. The main characters were still there.

The publisher that put it out had rejected it twice before over a period of seventeen years. But that third time was the charm. The timing finally hit. And it came out in the height of the Edwardian-story craze, which helped it to outsell everything else I've ever written and land itself on a bestseller list a year after it had first released. It was nominated for a Christy Award, and even now it remains one of my bestselling titles.

I certainly didn't just sit around and try to pitch that story year after year—I kept writing, kept working, kept pursuing other ideas. I published other books, I learned my craft. But I also never gave up on that first story that had seized my heart fully enough to make me hammer out a complete novel at age thirteen. And what a joy it was to finally hold it in my hands at age thirty-two!

The best piece of writing advice I ever got is so perfectly summed up by this story's story, and it's this: respect the dream. If writing is something you want to do, then you have to dedicate as much time and energy to it as you would any other career. You have to learn, you have to put in the hours, you have to admit where you're weak and figure out how to strengthen. You have to train, to learn the industry, and to pick yourself up after each rejection and failure. And when you do, then you never know how that dream will end up blooming. Sometimes in ways and with projects you never would have dreamed up at the start . . . and sometimes, those earliest dreams find their way into reality eventually too.

Roseanna M. White
www.RoseannaMWhite.com
Thirty-nine books published

Chapter 43

Stephanie Grace Whitson

A love for words and writing has always played an integral role in my life. My older siblings delighted in teaching me impressively long words. In school, I was the weird kid who loved writing assignments. I often think through problems by writing about them, tapping away on a keyboard and distanced from unhelpful emotions. That being said, I can't honestly say I ever aspired to become a novelist. But God . . .

In 1989, our home-schooling family moved to a Nebraska acreage. I'd grown up in Illinois, and so when it came time to teach Nebraska history, I learned along with my children. Fascinated by the lives of pioneer women, I began to read published diaries and reminiscences. Before long, I was writing scenes in the life of an imaginary woman named Jesse King (the name *King* borrowed from tombstones in an abandoned pioneer cemetery near our home). When a friend read those scenes, she insisted I finish the story. "I have to know what happens next."

At the time, our family had founded a home-based inspirational gift company. The Lord had blessed it, and hundreds of Christian bookstores nationwide carried gifts designed by Prairie Pieceworks. Finish Jesse's story? I couldn't just take time off from the business—unless I could sell the book, thereby continuing to contribute to the family budget.

The publishing world was not a complete unknown to me. Prior to having children, I had sold a couple of devotionals and a non-fiction article. I knew about the *Writers Market* guide and so I turned to it once again, selected three Christian fiction publishers, and sent off three query letters. I fully expected wholesale rejection, but things did not go as expected. Thomas Nelson Publishers requested sample chapters. I sent those off, flabbergasted a few weeks later when they requested the completed manuscript. I didn't have a completed manuscript!

Tempted to panic, I called the only other writer I knew for advice. She asked, "How long will it take you to finish the book?" I estimated six weeks. She encouraged me to respond to the publisher with that information and to get about finishing the book. Thomas Nelson said they would wait. I tried to finish the book, but the home-based business and family matters intervened. I didn't get the book finished.

Still expecting rejection, I decided to send the publisher what I had—about two-thirds of a book that included the beginning, the more dramatic scenes, and the ending. Where there was missing material, I inserted a blank sheet of paper on which I typed, "This chapter hasn't been written—here's what happens." The partial manuscript submitted, I went back to my life as the home-schooling mother of four running a home-based business. I didn't think much about the book. After all, there was no way a major publisher was going to buy a book based on a partial manuscript from a nobody.

One day after an outing into town, I returned home to a phone message I will never forget. "Stephanie, this is Lonnie Hull Dupont with Thomas Nelson Publishers. Please give me a call. I want to make you an offer we hope you won't refuse."

The initial shock worn off, my husband and I talked about what it would mean for me to sign a publishing contract. One obvious result would be that we'd need to close the home-based business. I couldn't possibly home school, run a business, and finish a book. Had our goals been met? We prayerfully decided that yes, they had. The children had learned budgeting, computer accounting and inventory control, and product design. They'd even run our booth at more than one major trade expo. At the family meeting that came next, the children agreed that they'd be happy to close the company down and let mom write her book. But another challenge emerged.

When Thomas Nelson's contract arrived, it wasn't for one book. It was for a three-book series. I remember staring at my husband in disbelief as I said, "I don't know if I can write three books. I haven't finished *one* yet." My practical husband replied, "They're paying you money. Sign the contract."

Walks the Fire came out in 1995. Editor Lonnie Hull Dupont proved to be a gift from God. She guided me toward developing my own voice. Her expertise put our first book on the CBA bestseller list. My career as a novelist was born.

If you have read this far, I hope my atypical "first book story" will encourage you to believe that *if God has a writing ministry for you, He can make it happen*. Looking back, I see His hand guiding and overcoming my mistakes. Everyone knows you need a completed, edited manuscript to get published—right? I know that, too—now. I also know that miracles happen and God uses the unexpected to provide for His own. I had several books in the Christian fiction marketplace when my husband, Bob, died of cancer. At the time, I had *no* marketable skills with which to support a family. I had been a French teacher, but I was not certified to teach in Nebraska. I had been a medical secretary, but I had none of the certifications required in 2001. What I did have was a young career as a novelist. Twenty-nine full length novels, four novellas, and twenty-nine years later, I'm still writing historical fiction.

The best piece of writing advice I ever got is this convicting quote from E. L. Doctorow: "Planning to write is not writing. Outlining a book is not writing. Researching is not writing. Talking to people about what you're doing, none of that is writing. Writing is writing."

Stephanie Grace Whitson
www.stephaniewhitson.com
Twenty-nine full length novels, four novellas published

Chapter 44

Brad Whittington

I started writing fiction in 1981 when I got a computer. Like a lot of other wannabes, what I wrote would best be described as "regrettable." Slowly, and I do mean slowly, I got better.

In the late 80s I made a brief attempt to get a kid's book published. It was about a precocious fifth-grade boy who wanted to be Sherlock Holmes and tried to turn everyone around him into the various secondary characters in Doyle's books. After several months, I realized I was spending all my free time managing submissions and rejections and not writing. I also realized that my odds of getting published were worse than winning the lottery. I decided to quit using my precious writing time doing what I hated (clerical work) and instead doing what I loved (writing).

I abandoned the thought of being published and continued to write, as I always had, for the sheer joy of writing. My main project was a collection of anecdotes from my high school and college days, which I titled

"Boring Stories." I printed them out on a dot matrix printer and gave copies to family and friends.

In 1991, my sister called to say that she had given my stories to a woman in her Sunday School class, Robin Hardy, who was a Christian romance novelist. (I didn't even know there was such a thing.) Robin wanted to chat with me the next time I was in town.

The meeting happened a few months later. She said she liked my writing, and if I could get the material into a final draft, she would pitch it to her editor. I did the rewrite, calling the new incarnation "Strange in a Stranger Land." Robin pitched it and it went nowhere. I forgot about it and continued to write for the joy of it.

I also changed careers (from education to technology) and spent the decade bouncing around from Texas to South Carolina, Arizona, Colorado, and eventually Hawaii, which is where I was living when Robin tracked me down in 2001.

It turned out that the reason my manuscript had gone nowhere a decade earlier was that the publisher was dropping their fiction line to focus on non-fiction. She had a new publisher and had shown the manuscript to her editor. He liked it and wanted to talk to me. Six months later I had a contract and a serious amount of work ahead of me to turn what was basically a first-draft collection of short stories into a publishable novel. A year later "Welcome to Fred," the first of four Fred books, hit the shelves and won a Christy award. That book is dedicated to Robin Hardy.

Maybe I should dust off that kid's book and see if it has any legs.

The best piece of writing advice I ever got: When you finish a book, start the next one. Don't sit around waiting to see what happens with the first one.

Brad Whittington
bradwhittington.com
Nine novels and two non-fiction books

Chapter 45

Jill Williamson

My entire childhood, I dreamed of becoming a fashion designer. I was obsessed with making and remodeling clothing. I knew the life story of every famous designer at the time. I attended the Fashion Institute of Technology in Manhattan, and after graduation, my husband and I moved to Los Angeles. Two unpleasant assistant designer jobs in the fashion industry and five years later, life was a bit like the book *The Devil Wears Prada*. My dream had turned out more like a nightmare.

I was pregnant with my first child, so I decided to stay home for a while. This gave me lots of time to think. My husband was a youth pastor, and I gravitated to the readers in the group. The teens shared their books with me, and I shared books with them. I started to think, "I should write a book for these teens. How hard could it be?"

The year was 2004. I decided to write a spy kid novel with a supernatural twist, like *Agent Cody Banks* meets Frank Peretti's *This Present Darkness*. To me, missionaries were real-life heroes, so I thought it would be fun to send my spy kids into foreign countries. I was an avid reader, but I knew nothing about plotting or character building or showing vs. telling. My big plan for structure (and please forgive me, because this was so silly) was to model my book after the Harry Potter books, since they were so popular at the time. That series has three main characters: two boys and a girl. The main boy character's parents died long ago. The girl is really smart. The three teens get sent away for "training" where they stumble into danger and ultimately save the day.

I used that for my characterization model and wrote a story about an orphan boy who gets recruited into a spy organization that's run by God. It's called The Mission League. God calls. The teens answer the call. They are in training and learn about things like spiritual gifts, spiritual warfare, and the identities of notorious cults in the world that need to be infiltrated and brought down.

I was hooked on my little story and having a blast writing it. When a writer's conference came to town, I signed up. I just KNEW that when the agent heard about my brilliant story it would be, "Move over J.K. Rowling, here I come!"

The keynote speaker was a highly respected literary agent named Steve Laube. He gave us all the opportunity to pitch to him during the break. My turn came and I said something like this:

"My story is about a kid named Spencer who plays basketball. He lives with his grandma because his parents died when he was little. He's really tall, and he likes eating peanut butter out of the jar. He gets recruited to be a spy, because there is this secret spy organization that sends kids out on missions, but regular people think they're going on mission trips—missionaries are my heroes, so I wanted to incorporate that somehow. Anyway, Spencer doesn't want to join these guys because he thinks they're crazy because he's not really a Christian, but he got in trouble at school, so his grandma makes him join. He goes to Moscow, and when he's there he stumbles onto this secret case with this evil lady who's trying to break into the field office. And Spencer keeps getting in trouble . . . "

I kept going. On and on and on and on . . . It's painful to recall.

Steve Laube's eyes started to glaze over. He was glancing over my shoulder to the line behind me, probably thinking, "Will she ever stop talking?" And, yes, I eventually did stop. And Steve said something like, "Yeah, well . . . Kids, they don't really like reading about missionaries. And young adult books don't really sell. I don't represent young adult authors for that very reason. The market is just too small."

So I said, "Oh. Okay. Thank you very much." And I walked away. Completely devastated.

I went up to my room and cried. Dreams crushed to ash! The reality check was a brutal shock, but when I had calmed down, I said to myself, "Okay. I know teens like my book because my youth group likes it. So, I must not have explained the story very well." (Ahem . . .) Then I thought, "Maybe if I finish the story all the way to the end, I would be able to explain it better." Because the book was only about 70% done at the time.

Then it hit me. I hadn't been respecting my dream!

I had respected my dream of becoming a fashion designer. I had taught myself to sew and remodel clothing. I had studied the industry and the competition. I went to college and earned a degree. I worked in the industry for five years.

But writing a novel? I had spent about five months on my spy kid story and had yet to finish a first draft, let alone edit the story. And I thought it was really to sell it without even bothering to put in the time to learn the craft of writing or how the publishing industry works or any of that. I wanted the dream without putting in the hard work.

I knew in that moment that I had two choices before me. I could quit and find something else to occupy my time, or I could keep at it, which would mean figuring out how to respect my dream of writing a novel.

I don't give up easily. And writing was really a lot of fun.

So I kept at it. I did everything Steve Laube said to do. I finished my novel. I found a critique group. I let them read my novel. I took their advice and rewrote my novel. I read books on the craft of writing and bought reference books to help me learn writing rules. I read other fiction books in my genre so that I would know what was selling already. I went to more writer's conferences. I queried other agents. I queried publishers. I wrote book two in the series. Then I wrote another book. And another book.

It took me four years before I was offered a book contract. But it wasn't for my spy novel, *The New Recruit*. Nope. It was for the book that became *By Darkness Hid* (Blood of Kings, book 1), which was the SIXTH novel I wrote!

Yep. The sixth book I wrote was my first traditionally published novel. Next, I started writing book two in the Blood of Kings trilogy. *By Darkness Hid* won a few awards, which got me an agent. Around that time, I opened up *The New Recruit* to have a look. (Because it was my baby, and I wanted to see it in print!) It had been over three years since I'd last looked at the manuscript, and when I read the first page, I thought, "Ug! This is not good. Not good at all!" I finally had enough writing experience under my belt that I was able to see what wasn't working. I completely rewrote the book, switching it from third person to first person. I found Spencer's voice, and he was hysterical!

My agent pitched the fifth book I'd written (*Replication*) and *The New Recruit* to Zondervan. They chose to offer me a contract for *Replication*. *The New Recruit* was rejected again!

After I finished writing the third Blood of Kings novel, I talked that same publisher into buying *The New Recruit*. It came out in 2012 and finaled for the American Christian Fiction Writers (ACFW) Carol Award. I was so happy! My publisher put out book two as well, which also finaled for a Carol Award, but then my publisher realized these books weren't really speculative. And since they published fantasy and science fiction, the series wasn't a great fit. He didn't want to publish the rest of the series. He said he could keep the first two in print and let me publish the others, or give me the rights back for the first two and then I could indie publish them all. It was up to me. So, I decided to indie publish the entire Mission League series, which is now complete with six books.

The best piece of writing advice I ever read was from Michael Crichton who said, "Books aren't written—they're rewritten. Including your own. It is one of the hardest things to accept, especially after the seventh rewrite hasn't quite done it."

This helped me a lot because I was trying to achieve perfection my first try, and that just wasn't realistic. I had to learn to give myself permission to write messy first drafts, knowing I'd be back to edit and refine the story later —knowing that messy is part of my process and that editing is important and necessary. That took off the pressure to be perfect and allowed me to find each story a lot faster.

Jill Williamson

www.jillwilliamson.com

Thirty-one books published to date.

Chapter 46

Kimberley Woodhouse

1995. A dark and stormy night in South Louisiana.

And my baby was sick.

Before we cue the angsty background track, let me give you a little context.

My husband and I both grew up in south *south* Louisiana. As in, if you lived north of I-10, you were considered <*gasp*> a northerner, you couldn't possibly know how to make jambalaya, étouffée, or gumbo properly, and you might actually use coffee that wasn't the Community brand.

Having never been north or west of Dallas, my sweet husband even told my father after graduating from Bible college that he would go wherever God called him . . . as long as it touched the Gulf of Mexico. (Yes, you are allowed to laugh . . . you probably know where this is going.)

Then there was me. Music was my life. Lessons, competitions, performances, accompanying, playing for church, singing in every ensemble and choir available. Basically everything I knew was music, reading, and full-time ministry. I had scholarships to Juilliard, the Chicago Conservatory of Music, LSU, and many others.

But I ended up at a little Bible college to study under a "retired" piano professor who—you've probably guessed—was from Juilliard. He'd been a concert pianist in the 1940s. As God's incredible plan would have it—I met the man who would become my husband at that little Bible college the very first day.

Fast forward several years. We were married and living on practically nothing in ministry. Our first baby arrived, and he kept getting sick. I stayed up with him and had this insatiable desire to *do* something with all the creative juices flowing through my mind.

Since waking up the neighborhood in the middle of the night playing and writing music was out of the question, I started writing stories. Lots of them.

And I didn't tell a single soul. Not even my husband. Because I was a musician. What did I know about writing stories?

Fast forward a few more years. We had two children, one of whom had been diagnosed with an extremely rare nerve disorder. She didn't sweat. Didn't feel pain the same way the rest of us do. The Lord—with His amazing sense of humor—decided to send this little southern family to the mission field in Alaska.

When Dad asked my husband about Alaska not touching the gulf—my husband was prepared with a grin. He shrugged, "All the water is connected."

It was this move to Alaska that became the true beginning to my writing career. My dear friend came over to help me pack but instead of actually doing that in the other room, she found my stories. After hours of reading them, she came into the room where I was packing box after box and proceeded to whack me over the head with a ream of paper. Then she threw it on the floor, placed her hands on her hips, and then told me in no uncertain terms that I was hiding my light under a bushel.

I have to admit, I sorta collapsed into a puddle of tears and whined that I didn't know a thing about writing. Music was what I knew.

She didn't buy my little pity-party. In fact, she held my toes to the fire and pushed me to look past my training and experience. To realize that I could rely on myself as much as I wanted, but what if God wanted to do something through me that was clearly *all* Him.

Everybody needs a friend like that. Because not only did she challenge me to step out of my comfort zone and my well-known-little-musician box, but she threatened my life if I didn't do something with my writing. My whole perspective changed about the gifts God had given me—and using my writing and music for Him and Him alone has been my goal.

Now, let's get one thing straight. I had a lot to learn about the craft. As in *everything*. I had tons of encouragement and mentoring from people in this very group (Chi Libris). Everyone told me I had the gift of a storyteller, but it took years to study, learn, and hone the craft. Let's be honest, I'm still learning. And relearning. And studying. And honing. And let's not forget editing. Lots and lots of editing.

I'm going to let you in on a secret. My very first full-length novel that I *wanted* to have published has actually *not* been published yet. In fact, my first published books ended up being non-fiction because of all the media surrounding our family's story. After that, publishers loved that I wanted to write about Alaska after living there for many years. My publishing journey has been unique just like so many others here. I'm okay with that.

Even as my fortieth book is set to release soon, I have thought about that first novel many times. Do I have enough know-how to edit the proverbial snot out of it and make it something worthy of publication? Or should it sit in the drawer—the first story of my heart?

I don't have the answer to that right now, but I do know one thing. God is the giver of story. He is *THE* Author. And if He has called you to write His stories, then don't you dare hide that light under a bushel. Or I might have to come visit and whack *you* over the head.

Keep on keepin' on.

> "Consider it pure joy, my brothers and sisters, whenever you face trials of many kinds, because you know that the testing of your faith produces perseverance. Let perseverance finish its work so that you may be mature and complete, not lacking anything."
> —James 1:2-4, NIV

Kimberley Woodhouse
kimberleywoodhouse.com
Forty-plus books

Chapter 47

Lenora Worth

I knew I wanted to write in the fourth grade. Our strict, stoic teacher assigned a writing project. I loved it and everyone else hated it. I knew from that moment I wanted to write stories. So I did. Wrote several melodramatic love stories of young angst and sold them on the playground for a quarter. I had a lot of milk money.

I wrote all through high school and while my teachers encouraged me and I won several writing contests, my family and others mostly patted me on the head and said, "That's nice, but you'll need a real job." So I took the typing class for writing books and to have something to fall back on. My senior year, my parents gave me a typewriter for Christmas, so they did understand my dream.

I got married, we had a daughter and we moved to from South Georgia to Atlanta where I worked in retail (my second career choice) and wrote when I could. A friend loaned me some romance novels and I decided I could write one of those, and so I began. But I wasn't ready to send that book to anyone. When I finally did, it got rejected and I was devastated. But I didn't give up.

We moved to Louisiana for my husband's work, and one day I was in a shopping mall (because shoes) and saw several local authors signing books. Romance authors. They invited me to join their writers group. From there, I learned how to write and I also learned the business of writing, and a few years and many rejections later, after we'd had our second child, I finally sold a contemporary romance to Avalon. I was in bed with the flu and when I got the call, I though it was a telemarketer and almost hung up.

But the nice voice on the line said, "No, don't hang up. We want to buy your book."

Well, I listened and agreed and then I thought, "I must have died and gone to heaven. This can't be real."

It was real. That same morning I'd ordered some ink cartridges for my husband to pick up on the way home. And I told the nice lady there that I'd finally sold a book to a publisher. She was so excited, she blurted it out to my husband and when he came home, he thought I was so sick I was hallucinating. I told him it was true. Avalon sold mostly to libraries, so my advance was six-hundred-dollars. Since that day I've been writing consistently for thirty years, mostly for Love Inspired. But remember that first book that got rejected? That finally became my fiftieth book for Harlequin. It was a sweet Super-romance. Now, with over a hundred books and novellas published, I still love the thrill of getting the call— "We want to buy your book."

I wasn't hallucinating! I have a real job and I love it.

The best advice I've ever heard: Don't compare yourself to others. And I might add what I tell people when I do workshops. Don't say I want to be the next Karen Kingsbury. Be the first you! Karen is amazing, but you need to find your voice and your style and your place in publishing. Be the first you! Because your stories will be uniquely yours. That's the joy of writing.

Lenora Nazworth, writing as Lenora Worth
lenoraworth.com
100+ books published

Also by the Novelists of ChiLibris

The Storytellers' Collection, Volume 1: Tales of Faraway Places

The Storytellers' Collection, Volume 2: Tales from Home

What the Wind Picked Up: Proof that a Single Idea Can Launch a Thousand Stories

A Novel Idea: Best Advice on Writing Inspirational Fiction

Made in the USA
Columbia, SC
19 January 2024